THE PATHWAY OF PEACE

T0382318

LECTURES DELIVERED ON THE
SIR GEORGE WATSON FOUNDATION
FOR AMERICAN HISTORY, LITERATURE,
AND INSTITUTIONS

THE
PATHWAY OF PEACE

AN INTERPRETATION OF
SOME BRITISH-AMERICAN CRISES

by

ROBERT McELROY

PH.D., LL.D., M.A. (OXON), F.R.HIST.S.

*Fellow of Queen's College, Oxford; Harold Vyvyan Harmsworth
Professor of American History in Oxford University;
Sometime Edward's Professor of American History
in Princeton University*

WITH AN INTRODUCTION

by

THE RT HON. H. A. L. FISHER
Warden of New College, Oxford

CAMBRIDGE
AT THE UNIVERSITY PRESS
1927

CAMBRIDGE
UNIVERSITY PRESS

University Printing House, Cambridge CB2 8BS, United Kingdom

Published in the United States of America by Cambridge University Press, New York

Cambridge University Press is part of the University of Cambridge.

It furthers the University's mission by disseminating knowledge in the pursuit of education, learning and research at the highest international levels of excellence.

www.cambridge.org
Information on this title: www.cambridge.org/9781107646971

First published 1927
First paperback edition 2014

A catalogue record for this publication is available from the British Library

ISBN 978-1-107-64697-1 Paperback

To

MY MOTHER

INTRODUCTION

THESE clear and readable lectures constitute an attempt to set out the progress of that mutual understanding between the American and British governments which has now been ripened by a hundred and thirteen years of unbroken peace. In the compass of a small volume Professor McElroy cannot, of course, retrace in all its stages, the diplomatic history of Anglo-American relations since the Declaration of Independence. All that he can hope to do is to touch lightly upon certain typical episodes and to comment upon their significance. This task he has achieved in that spirit of critical detachment which we have now happily learned to expect from the historians who are trained in the Universities of the United States. That his sentiments are thoroughly friendly to Great Britain and to the improvement of the existing good relations between the two English-speaking Democracies will not render his work less acceptable on this side of the Ocean and will, I trust, be regarded as no detraction from its value by his own fellow-countrymen. For in the realm of politics there are two broad propositions which no man of sense will challenge. One is the surpassing importance to the well-being of human

society of Anglo-American co-operation; the
other, which is correlative, the catastrophe to
the whole fabric of civilization which would
result from a rupture of the Anglo-American
peace.

H. A. L. FISHER

30 *January* 1927

CONTENTS

Chapter I

THE INTERNATIONAL MIND

The Sage, Confucius, when dying, asked to be carried to the door of his house in Shantung, that he might take a farewell look at the world. And he wept over its condition. If that ancient philosopher were to return to-day, and survey the wider, though ever narrowing world, would he dry his tears? Twenty-four centuries of loam have gathered upon his simple grave in China's sacred peninsula, and still what the world is looking for is eternal peace. What she is looking at is almost eternal war. Still men fight one another for the love of God, fight one another for the love of gain.

For the unnumbered centuries since human society began, men charged with political leadership have searched with eager longing for one formula: a substitute for war. They have tried alliances, negotiations, economic pressure, isolation, agreements to arbitrate. But in the fullness of time each of these formulas has failed: and again and again unwilling as well as willing warriors have been forced back, or have joyfully returned, to war as their very unsafe rock of defence.

It would, however, be the philosophy of despair to say that to-day we are where our ancestors started, in the dim shadowland of history. It is beyond question that alliances, negotiations, economic pressure, isolation and agreements to arbitrate have, in many instances, enabled nations to avoid war. It is certain that, by their use, we have made progress toward more general peace: but it is equally obvious that the end of war is not yet. The world is still short of metal for ploughshares and pruning hooks because it must still have swords and spears.

Peace is far easier to abolish than war, not because any nation loves war more than peace, but because war may come from the will to war on the part of one: but peace only comes from the will to peace on the part of all. "It takes two to make a quarrel," says an ancient proverb: but one nation with a will to war can make a war.

In seeking to solve a problem, one's first concern is always with the question of method. The method of ending war by fighting for peace has been tried, and found at best only measurably successful; though the late Peace of Paris, with all of its faults, promises perhaps a greater measure of success, as it was the result of negotiations representing more thought for the people of the various nations than had any previous negotiations of truly international proportions. Likewise, the method of refusing to fight for peace, when need seemed to demand the thrust of steel, has failed. Military preparedness has not brought peace; military unpreparedness has proved, like an un-fenced sheepfold on the mountain, an invitation to every rambling beast of prey. Certainly there remain to-day few in any land with full faith in the efficacy of either method, though in every land there remain some who still cry these ancient, badly damaged wares.

In a certain ancient controversy, St Paul summed up the vanity of the arguments of both sides by the words: "Circumcision availeth nothing, neither uncircumcision; but a new creature." And it is fair to adapt his words to our problem and say: "Neither militarism availeth anything, nor paci-fism, but a new vision."

What that new vision is may be stated in the words of America's greatest legal mind, Elihu Root, who once said: "The indispensable pre-requisite of lasting peace is the creation of the international mind." And by that he meant nothing calculated to detract from the glory and dignity of the nation; but rather something calculated immeasurably to increase them. The international mind means higher loyalty to principles than to places, to ideals than to persons. It looks upon a nation's heritage of freedom, not as a possession to be hoarded, but as a trust to be executed. Such inheritances cannot belong: what we have of freedom, of power, of enlightenment, we hold in trust for all humanity. This is true, not of America alone, not of America and England alone, not of the West alone, but of all nations.

The international mind is not the enemy of the nation, but its ally. It comes not to destroy patriotism but to glorify it. It is therefore entitled to a welcome from every nation whose aim is justice and whose method, law. Too many well-intending patriots are content with a patriotism which says: "My country right or wrong," heedless of the obvious fact that true patriotism can never demand allegiance to error and to crime. And too many, in every nation, are hourly being taught the old foolish dream of national or race supremacy. The man who thinks his race born to rule other races, and teaches his children so, is not a friend to peace. He is her enemy: for unity based upon any form of human bondage is the vainest of delusions. We are, and we should wish to remain, Americans or English, French or German, Japanese, Chinese, Siamese, or whatever God has

4

seen fit to make us. But we must be free, when "unity all-pervading" comes at last.

Toward that guiding star of all the world, Liberty, each race must struggle. This is not an ideal, abstract, artificial, within the power of each to hold, or cast aside. It is an instinct, one of the world's great, unifying instincts, which all must recognize, or pay the heavy price of ceaseless wars. Lincoln was but paying it his tribute when he said: "I love my country, partly because it is my country, but chiefly because it is a free country."

The international mind seeks not supremacy but unity: and international unities are many and of transcendent importance in the search for a formula for lasting peace. Aristotle, whom Dante called "the master of them that know," distinguished 'essential' qualities which distinguish men from all other created beings, and 'incidental' qualities which distinguish men as individuals. Thus he conceived men as alike in what must be, but different in what may be. But the things which make men alike are more important than the things which make them different, and the international mind dwells upon the things which make men alike.

When we add the characteristic Aristotelian generalization: "What is most known is most real," we have the key to the provincial mind, the mind which dwells on the things which make men different. Men know best their own nations, their own races, their own localities, and very little of those which are distant. Therefore, the known things being for them the real things, they attach to local matters, local interests, local customs, pre-judices, or pre-suppositions, an exaggerated importance. All rational minds must deal with both essentials and incidentals, with the things which make men alike and the things which make them different; but the international mind sees more clearly than the provincial mind the superior importance of essentials as compared with incidentals. The international mind appreciates the importance of wider unities; the provincial mind concentrates its attention upon divergences, and resents the suggestion that recognition of wider unities is desirable.

Our present conception of the essential unities between races and nations is as vague as was that of American national unity a century and a half ago, perhaps even more vague. But as the milestones pass they indicate progress. The sense of unity, once limited to areas called states, and later extended to areas called nations, now begins to touch the horizon. But old conceptions yield

6

slowly, at times sullenly, to newer, broader conceptions: and it would be absurd to believe that international chaos will suddenly yield to international unity. The truly educated, of every nation, however, owes to the advancing vision, the dawning international mind, this much at least, a vow to think of every question in the largest possible terms. Viscount Grey was right when he said: "the large view will bring them (men) together, where the small view has separated them." And the formula which will some day show the substitute for war, will embody the large view, because it must meet the conditions, not of one nation, but of all nations.

The basic difficulties which each nation faced in discovering the essential unities which made it a nation are the basic difficulties which every other nation has had to face in seeking that same end; the same which the nations of the world must face in discovering the world-wide unity upon which alone real International Law can be established. And chief among these was and is the provincial mind.

The Romans complacently declared: "All roads lead to Rome"; and they measured all distances in their so-called World Empire from one golden column erected in their own Forum. To-day we begin to see that all roads lead to "the unity all-pervading": but there is no golden column to show us the exact centre of that new unity. In consequence, each nation is crying, "Lo; here it is, in the centre of our nation. Measure from that!" Thus we have as many centres as we have sovereign nations, and each, for its own people, is the centre of organized society, a centre which they stand ready to insist upon, by force if necessary. This is not a criticism: it is a statement of fact, inevitable to a certain stage in a great progress.

The determination of justice by the exhibition of major force was a rational theory so long as men believed that God gave to justice always the major force: but it is supremely irrational now that men have ceased to believe that God has so organized His world: and it becomes absurd when those who have impiously eliminated God from the picture continue to employ the terms of the old theory. Without God in the world, it is reasonable for men to elevate mere physical force to His despoiled throne: but to pretend that they fight to establish the right then becomes only a grim jest. The only logic of such a situation is the logic which gives to force the right to rule by virtue of its physical power. To pretend to any other virtue is to mock intelligence.

Yet, everywhere and always, men organized into small unities have shown and still show a tendency to fight against the creation of larger unities. If we take America as an example, we find this tendency to have been the very centre of her history. The conscious aim of the American Revolution was not the creation of a nation, and America persistently refused to be a nation when the war was over. Each State was intent upon the preservation of the Government which it had already developed, and upon the preservation of what John Bassett Moore calls its "personality in International Law." Supremely local, supremely self-conscious, it was as fearful of central control from a central American Government as it had been resentful of Parliamentary pretensions to supremacy. To picture the American Revolution as an attempt to erect a new nation is to write inverted history. The American patriots fought to protect their local Governments, and the struggle produced conditions which forced nationality upon them. The creation of the nation was a slow and painful process, an unwilling yielding to the imperious demands of necessity, not the eager following of an ideal of "Liberty and Union, now and forever one and inseparable," as it slowly became. John Adams was writing sound history

9

when he declared that the Constitution was "extracted from a reluctant people by grim necessity."

Before the new form which we call the American nation emerged, it was necessary that new unities, common interests not before discerned, should become evident, not only to the few, but to the many. A people which had thought in the political form called the State had to learn to think in terms of a larger unit called the Nation, and that could be no sudden process.

The years which followed the Revolutionary war, and which terminated with the adoption of the Constitution of 1789, are crowded with examples of this tendency to fight against the creation of a larger unity: which tendency is also the keynote of America's Civil War.

The Civil War has been so interpreted as to cause the average American to look upon the Southern States as a unique instance of localism: but in its localism the South was by no means unique. The eleven States which had recourse to arms against the larger unit, in the belief that by secession they would protect the smaller units, were merely belated instances of a localism once shared by all sections of America, a localism which each in turn had stood ready to defend when threats of central control seemed to menace especially cherished rights and privileges. All Americans now know, and freely admit, the truth of the words of Elihu Root: "The preservation of our duel system of government...has made possible our growth in local self-government and national power in the past, and...is essential to the continuance of that Government in the future."

It would be folly to draw world-lessons from one passing tale: but history shows innumerable instances which illustrate the inevitable cost of local thinking: and the world to-day is endangering her hope of peace by thinking once more in sections, dreaming again local dreams. Wisdom demands that we judge the future by means of the past. Because America has developed a national mind out of a people representing all races and kindreds and tongues: and because Great Britain has similarly given a British mind to millions of her far-flung Empire, we believe that the same process of discovering unity in diversity may yet result in the creation of an international mind, which will think in common ethical terms, accept common standards of conduct, and thus make possible a wide range of laws of world-wide operation.

But it has taken one hundred and fifty years for America to understand that her people are more secure in their vital liberties as one sovereign nation than they could ever have been as citizens of thirteen sovereign States: and it will require the long patience which the French proverb calls genius to make the nations of the world understand that the vital liberties of their people will at last be more secure under an all-pervading unity sustained by International Law than they could ever be as citizens of fifty odd sovereign nations, standing each alone.

Chapter II

An American novelist was once asked by a re-
porter whether writing novels was hard work.
His unhesitating answer was: "All work is hard
work"; and we may say with equal truth: "All
international problems are hard problems." Those,
however, which prove more than normally difficult erect themselves into monuments of wisdom,
or folly, and take their places in history as international crises.

The aim of diplomacy is two-fold, to prevent
international crises where they may be prevented,
and to solve them by methods of reason when they
cannot be prevented. Diplomacy begins as soon
as a nation is acknowledged as sovereign, and continues until reason prepares to give place to force:
its agents are the nation's diplomats: and the
treaties, conventions and other agreements which
these diplomats make embody, and must embody,
not the law of one nation alone, but the law which
each nation stands ready to accept, and to abide by.

An accumulation of accepted custom regulating
the intercourse of nations, and called International

Law, defines the unities already discovered, and
these bind every civilized nation, being explicitly
or tacitly accepted when a nation is admitted into
the family of nations. When, for example, with
the adoption of the Federal Constitution of 1789,
the United States became a responsible nation
among the nations of the world, the question was
raised: "Does this customary law of nations bind
her?" Alexander Hamilton, in No. 20 of his
Letters of Camillus gave the answer which his
nation fully accepted:

The United States, when a member of the
British Empire, were, in this capacity, a party to
that law, and not having dissented from it, when
they became independent, they are to be considered as having continued a party to it. The
common law of England, which was and is in
force in each of these states, adopts the law of
nations,...as a part of itself. Ever since we have
been an independent nation, we have appealed to
and acted upon the modern law of nations as
understood in Europe—various resolutions of
Congress during our revolution, the correspondence of executive officers, the decisions of our
Courts of Admiralty, all recognised this standard.
Executive and legislative acts, and the proceedings
of our Courts, under the present Government,
speak a similar language....It is indubitable that
the customary law of European nations is a part

14

of the Common law, and, by adoption, that of the United States.

But the task of the diplomat extends beyond the mere acceptance of recognized International Law. His task is also the discovery of new unities between his nation and that to which he is accredited. This duty, difficult in itself, is made far more difficult, in the case of American diplomats, by reason of certain dominant conditions, which, for the hundred and thirty-seven years since the American Federal experiment began, have been present, though in varying proportions, in every British-American crisis. There is no British-American treaty in all those years which has not been affected by them. No American statesman, sent to deal with Great Britain, has been able to make his plans without the obtrusive consciousness of their presence, and their mighty power—for weal or woe. These conditions are difficult to define: but a clear understanding of them is essential to the work of discovering new unities between these two nations.

Traditional Misunderstanding of the American Revolution. The first may be described as a traditional misunderstanding of the American Revolution. For the century and a half since the Declaration of Independence the printing press, through text books on American history, has served up to each generation of Americans, of myriad races and racial inheritances, an interpretation of the American Revolution which sound American scholarship has so far been unable completely to unhorse. The American patriot of 1776 looked upon the American loyalist of 1776 as the willing vassal of a despot's throne, upon King George III as the very prince of tyrants, and upon England as a nation bent upon making slaves of her colonists.

Likewise for the building of fighting machines in England it was essential that Englishmen at home should learn to think of Americans, then overwhelmingly Anglo-Saxon in blood, as "black-hearted fellows," whom one would not care to meet in the dark, or as "a race of convicted felons," to quote the eloquence of Dr Johnson. They were led to see the church-born Committees of Correspondence as "the foulest, subtlest, and most venomous serpent ever issued from the egg of sedition": and America was pictured as a place where the King's enemies went about in homespun, and his friends in tar and feathers.

Such interpretations, absurd as we know them to have been, then seemed essential to the task of kindling the hatred necessary to convert friends into foes, and brothers into conscientious executioners. And, so long as war continues periodically to ravage the human sheepfold (and only sublime faith can foresee its end), so long will men indulge in a propaganda, whose aim is action rather than truth. In our saner moments we do not defend this policy, but in our insaner moments all nations practise it, consciously or unconsciously.

To carry such misinformation over into days of peace, to perpetuate as history fictions begotten by war is clearly folly. Yet, in the case of the American Revolution we carried our anti-British propaganda as history for over a century; and only now are we relinquishing it in favour of real history. The bare facts are interesting, and fortunately available. In 1917 Charles Altschul published a pamphlet entitled: *The American Revolution in our School Text-Books*, based upon a careful, statistical study of the facts.

Taking forty American Histories, widely used twenty years ago in American schools throughout the nation, he arranged them in five groups according to the fairness, measured by present scholarly opinion, of their interpretation of the Revolution of 1776. His general conclusion is in these words:

The great majority of History text books, used in our Public Schools more than 20 years ago, gave a very incomplete picture of general political conditions in England prior to the American Revolution, and either did not refer at all to the great efforts made by prominent Englishmen in behalf of the Colonies, or mentioned them only casually.

The number of popular text books thus defective and misleading was not only much larger than those fairer in treatment, but far more widely and generally used. "The public mind (then in school but now in control of the nation)," he adds, "must thereby have been prejudiced against England."

In general, it is fair to say that the popular estimate of a neighbour's righteousness depends most upon early education. Early education regarding the attitude of other nations toward our own depends chiefly upon the elementary text book: and these were commonly written, twenty years ago, not by the scholar who had won his opinion by a life-time study of the records, but by experienced teachers who followed after the traditional treatment, having neither the time nor the training to study the facts in the large range of topics which they must serve up to the potential minds of a nation. In consequence, with no desire or purpose to perpetuate error, or to be the means of erecting barriers against normal international friendship, the text book writers of each generation handed down to the next a tale that was told, rather than a judicial interpretation of facts with propaganda of earlier days properly eliminated. Thus generation after generation saw Englishmen through enemy eyes, and drank in belated propaganda with expanding youthful minds, and the easy susceptibilities of youth.

To remove from history the propaganda of the past is an important part of the duty of the historian. And it is a duty which often requires both knowledge and courage. To remove from the text books of any people loved legends which have lingered too long is analogous to the task of robbing a lioness of her whelps: and many a courageous historian knows that all too well. But, in the face of bitter attacks, cries of "unpatriotic conduct" from the unknowing, and imputation of other unworthy motives, American historians have persisted in the effort to get out of our text books the revolutionary propaganda which has been long employed for the spiritual feeding of the rising generations. And they have, in large measure, succeeded. Mr Altschul's conclusion, from the study of fifty-three American History text books now widely used, is in these words:

The children now studying American History in the Public (free) Schools have a far greater number of text books available which give relatively complete information on this subject.

By this he does not mean that our text books are as yet wholly freed from the evils just described: but at least our children are now being taught the great truth that the American Revolution was a struggle in both countries of the reactionary elements against the progressive elements. They are taught, from the first, to understand that not all of the Fathers of the Republic dwelt in America: but that Chatham, Fox, Burke, Barré, Rockingham, Wilkes, Shelburne, and a host of other British leaders of the day were, in a very real sense, also "Fathers of the Republic."

Since the accession of the Shelburne ministry there has been no cause for Americans and British to quarrel over the Revolution: for we have viewed the chief issues from the same standpoint. And that common viewpoint has been made ever more apparent as the generations have passed. With the progress of Parliamentary reform in England, the vision of the British Fathers of the American Revolution has slowly melted into reality: and that reality has gradually permeated the British Empire, transforming it into the present British

Commonwealth of Nations. The eminent Oxford historian of the British Constitution, Professor A. V. Dicey, thus interprets the change:

Parliament...long before 1884 practically admitted the truth of the doctrine in vain pressed upon his contemporaries by Burke, when insisting upon the folly of the attempt made by the Parliament of England to exert as much absolute power in Massachusetts as in Middlesex, that a real limit to the exercise of Sovereignty is imposed not by the laws of man but by the nature of things; and that it is vain for a parliament or any other sovereign to try to exert equal power throughout the whole of an immense Empire. The completeness of this admission is shown by one noteworthy fact: the Imperial Parliament in 1884, and long before 1884, had ceased to impose its own authority, and for the benefit of England, any tax upon any British colony. The omnipotence, in short, of Parliament, though theoretically admitted, has been applied in its full effect only to the United Kingdom.

With the progress of Parliamentary reform, and of self-government in the vanishing Empire of Great Britain, the United States and the British Commonwealth of Nations began ever more fully to acknowledge a common Sovereign, not a Tudor, a Stuart or a Hanoverian, but the Sovereign People. But still, though in rapidly lessening measure, it is true that behind all British-American crises is an inherited spirit of feud, a detailed knowledge of the things which count against British-American friendship, and little or no knowledge of the things which should bind these two nations together in friendly sympathy.

America's Racial Complex. A second condition at the back of all British-American diplomacy, of whatever period, is America's racial complex. Since the *Susan Constant,* the *Godspeed,* and the *Discovery* sailed from the Downs, on December 20, 1606, with 105 potential Americans aboard, bound, as Captain John Smith prophetically said, for a land where the only drink was water and the dwellings castles in the air, every race of God's creation has made its home in America. And with each came the call of blood, which seems to be a part of every man. Men may leave their country for conscience, for adventure, for a chance of gain, for the avoidance of ills grown too heavy to bear. They may leave their country for their country's good, or in quest of quiet. There are a thousand lures in every frontier land: but with each pilgrim, adventurer or crusader, there goes the memory of another land where lies the dust of a hundred generations of ancestors from whom he sprang. And no new devotion to a new land—however great that devotion—can ever make that new land the only vision of his lonely hours, or prevent his telling to his sons, and his sons' sons the stories of the old homeland from which he came, and idealizing it. And "the old home" now means not England only, as in early days, but every land on which the sun shines, or refuses to shine. America is of the blood of all the world: and she will miss her destiny unless she tunes her thoughts to the pulse of all humanity. Every race has lent its golden tissues for the weaving of the fabric which we call America.

Americans of whatever blood, seeing America in danger, respond, regardless of race, creed or country, putting America first. But with reference to questions purely European, each instinctively thinks Polish, Italian or Irish, Greek, Russian or German, according to his racial background, even as the Anglo-Saxon instinctively thinks English. And this is a fact which no American statesman can forget, and live, politically: for with thought in terms of race, or blood, the shades of ancient wrongs, forgotten prejudices, begin to walk abroad, haunting new generations. Then forgotten lessons of early text books return, not as concrete facts, but as spiritual prejudices, the most difficult of all factors in statesmanship.

This condition at the back of American diplomatic problems is nothing new. It is an old condition intensified by years of immigration. Father Joques visited Manhattan Island in 1643 and reported four hundred men living within sight of the Battery, and speaking all told eighteen languages; since when there have never been less, but always more and more, until to-day a brief walk on the east side of New York City at noon will show one all the nations of the earth in a moment of time: and the Tower of Babel seems strangely near at hand.

Nor is the polyglot character of America's population confined to Manhattan Island. It is nationwide. When the Great War began there were in the United States two hundred daily newspapers printed in German; one hundred and ten in Italian; one hundred and twenty in the Scandinavian tongues; and it is said that the war was proclaimed in Chicago alone in forty-seven languages. In a recent book called *Race or Nation*, Gino Speranza assures us that "in 1920, out of a white population of about 95,000,000, nearly 14,000,000 were born in forty-five different countries, and 23,000,000 more were of foreign or half-foreign parentage." It is true that of the 14,000,000 *foreign-born* those of British birth, Canadians, Irish, English and Scotch, greatly outnumber *any other single group*. It is also true that about 50 per cent. of the *American-born* white population is still of British origin: but the percentage of British blood in the total population has steadily diminished as compared with this vast combination of other bloods representing the tide of immigration of a century and a half.

But, though the Briton's relative, numerical strength has diminished, his spiritual influence remains. British blood still continues to furnish a preponderating proportion of American leadership. Every President, save Van Buren and Roosevelt, has been of British stock; and British institutions still hold their ancient dominion, not because they are British, but because the American people, regardless of race, consider them best; a tribute the sincerity of which is none the less real because unconscious.

Such a racial complex demands of the American Government the most scrupulous avoidance of both race prejudice and race favouritism. Even in Washington's time this was so evident that in his Farewell Address to the American people he declared, as part of his legacy of experience: "Nothing is more essential than that permanent and inveterate antipathies against particular nations, and passionate attachments for others, should be excluded." And this is even truer to-day—Personally, I, (being any individual American) may prefer an Englishman to a Russian Jew, a Scandinavian to an Italian; but as an American citizen I must insist that my Government shall cherish no such preference: for its only chance of unity is an impartial affection for all of its citizens, of whatever race, whether Americans by right of birth, or by that of choice.

Anti-Imperialism. A third element at the back of British-American relations is the fact that every American, from the cradle to the grave, is trained to distrust and abhor what he calls *Imperialism.* He learns, with pride, that America has increased her original territory five-fold: but he never thinks of that vast expansion as even remotely imperialistic. The reason is plain, and sound: throughout the history of American expansion there has existed one fact, not always apparent in European expansion. America, up to 1898, gave to all of her territory, whether won by purchase alone, or by purchase aided by conquest, exactly the same rights, privileges and immunities which belonged to the older sections. This policy was not decided upon without opposition, without the lamentations of prophets of evil, without the fear of disastrous consequences; but it was decided upon. To every foot of soil beneath her flag she, in good faith, delivered representative government and perfect equality, as rapidly as controlling circumstances allowed. Under the Ordinance of 1787, which provided the machinery for territorial assimilation, Americans have looked upon new dependencies as potential States, charges in training for the full duties of free government: and, conscious of their own rectitude in this respect, they have been prone for generations to interpret other forms of expansion as the exploitation of helpless souls: from whence has arisen no small part of the suspicion with which America has regarded European conferences.

The acquisition, however, of extra-continental dependencies, by the Spanish war of 1898, somewhat modified America's point of view. She now sees that there are problems and problems, and understands that dominion over backward peoples may involve issues which did not appear during the century of American expansion within her own Continent. She has learned that the principle of self-determination has limits which have not always been set by the selfishness of dominant nations, but often by their unselfishness. In spite of this fact, however, America's ancient suspicion of European imperialism is still a controlling factor in her diplomacy.

27

The Advice and Consent of the Senate. The fourth dominant condition at the back of all American diplomacy is of an entirely different character, but its clear understanding is no less necessary to the harmony which will make easier important international agreements: namely, the fact that all American agreements with other nations, by whomsoever signed, must in the end be subject to the acceptance, alteration or rejection of the United States Senate.

Obviously, under any form of popular government, the executive power must fall short of the ability to bind a nation beyond the people's will; for the existence of executive power not so limited would in itself constitute a proof that the Government in question was not a popular government. The difference between popular governments lies, therefore, only in the machinery adapted to insure popular control. In England the Foreign Office is so organized as to be able to meet foreign emergencies without formal action by Parliament. The American system, however, is quite different. The Fathers of the American Constitution, in obedience to the demands of a then dominantly local patriotism, designed a government of checks and balances, giving to the Federal Executive control of pending diplomatic negotiations, and to the States, speaking through the Senate (a Council of the States' ambassadors) the right to accept, reject or alter his tentative agreements. In consequence no person or group of persons, except the United States Senate, has ever been able to say in advance how far the Executive may speak for the American nation: and it matters not at all whether the President speaks in person, or through the organized department known as the Department of State.

The Constitution of the United States, in Article II, Section 2, Clause 2, declares: "He (The President) shall have power, by and with the *Advice and Consent of the Senate*, to make treaties, provided two-thirds of the Senators present concur." And Mr Justice Story, in his *Commentaries*, explains the clause in these words:

The power to make treaties is general, and, of course, it embraces treaties for peace, or war; for commerce, or cessions of territory; for alliance, or succour; for indemnity for injuries, or payment of debts; for the recognition or establishment of principles of public law; and for any other purposes, which the policy, necessities, or interests of independent nations may dictate. Such a power is so large, and so capable of abuse, that it ought not to be confined to any one man, nor even to a mere majority of any public body, in a republican

29

government. There should be some higher pledge for the sound policy or necessity of a treaty. It should receive, therefore, the sanction of such a number of public functionaries, as would furnish a sufficient guarantee of such policy or necessity. Two-thirds of the Senate, therefore, are required to give validity to a treaty.

There can be no doubt that, in this paragraph, the great commentator fairly presents the mind of the Convention of 1787 which drafted the American Constitution. With the single exception of the principle of local self-government, no ideal was dearer to the hearts of that Assembly than the principle that in the determination of foreign relations the States as States should have the controlling voice. "They were," says James M. Beck, in his brilliant volume, *The Constitution of the United States*, "as little inclined to permit the President of the United States to make treaties or declare war at will in their behalf, as the European nations would be to-day to vest a similar authority in the League of Nations." Their jealous insistence upon the protection of existing local rights made them extremely suspicious of all centralizing tendencies, and they clung stubbornly to the principle of local control of foreign relations until the Connecticut delegation, speaking through

Benjamin Franklin, the Nestor of the Convention, proposed the so-called Connecticut Compromise which offered to the States, represented as States in the Senate, a veto upon the decisions of the more popular House of Representatives. The compromise gave to the States as States a grateful sense of security: and it at first looked as though this council of the States' ambassadors would be given full and exclusive control of foreign affairs. But, in view of the fact that the Senate would be often in recess, it was finally agreed to allow the ever-active Executive power to negotiate treaties, reserving to the Senate the right to step in and review his work before it received the power to bind.

As a natural corollary to that final control of foreign agreements came a similar control of the choice of the instruments through which the Executive should negotiate. Thus *the Advice and Consent of the Senate* was made applicable both to the making of treaties and to the appointment of ambassadors, other public ministers and consuls.

President Washington, at the very beginning of the Federal Government, adopted the policy of consulting the Senate in advance with reference to projects involving foreign nations. Unfortunately, that policy was soon abandoned. It has, however, generally been the practice of Presidents to keep in close touch with the Senate while foreign negotiations were in progress: and thus most Presidents have been able to form in advance a fairly reliable opinion as to whether a projected agreement would, in the end, be accepted by the Senate. But when a President has ventured to make international promises, or to form international agreements, without soliciting the *advice* of the Senate, he has frequently found the *consent* of the Senate as difficult to secure as the traditional pot of gold at the end of the rainbow.

The operation of this *Advice and Consent of the Senate* clause of the Constitution has done the nation some good, and some evil: but quite regardless of the question, *which* has dominated— the good results or the evil results—it has been one of the constant conditions at the back of all our diplomacy. Wherever American diplomats, special commissioners, or executive agents, have met at the green baize tables the representatives of other nations, they have done so with the full consciousness that they did not share with St Peter the power to "bind on earth."

Of all permanent conditions at the back of American diplomacy this Senatorial control of foreign affairs has of late years elicited the most hostile criticism from foreign countries. But such criticism has been due not to a constitutional defect but rather to the failure of various American Executives to make certain that their plans and promises were consistent with the views of the Senate.

This joint control of foreign relations, furthermore, insures that every commitment of the American Government will be brought out into the clear light of day. Executive sessions of the Senate may keep secret certain processes while they are in progress: but in American foreign relations there is nothing hid that shall not be revealed, and what is spoken in the ear must straightway be proclaimed upon the house top. Secret treaties are, for the United States of America, impossibilities.

The Glory of a Common Vision. But, while each of the thirty-nine American ministers and ambassadors, who have been accredited to the Court of St James since our Federal Constitution was adopted, has faced his tasks surrounded by the hampering limitations of the three forces: an outworn propaganda, a racial complex, and a senatorial control of foreign affairs, each has also had ever-present one factor not given to our diplomats in other lands. The bond between England and America, wrote Alfred Noyes, "is wider and deeper than mere relationship to two clans of seafaring pirates, the over-discussed Angles and Saxons." Despite our many differences, advancing knowledge will one day convince a sceptical world that there is an Anglo-American unity higher than blood kinship, higher than economic interest, namely, a common faith in the world-wide applicability of the institutions which have given to these two nations the spiritual leadership of a disheartened world.

In 1889 the historian, von Holst, wrote: "The Constitution of the United States has been the political bible of the people...the fetish...raised up for the worship of the masses by their leaders: and the masses in turn compelled their leaders to fall down and adore it." And, in scorn, he added: It is "a ruinous idolatry in which the idol worshipped was themselves."

But the idol worshipped is not themselves. Their worship of the Constitution leads the spirits of all Americans, of whatever race, back and back, to the dawn of England's heroic struggle for free institutions, against all foes, foreign or domestic. And as their quickened memories scan the pages of that thrilling history, they know in truth that their Constitution is the first fruits of Anglo-Saxon planting. They know that they are not false historians who paint English history as a long, long conflict for human freedom: and, with all of America's industrial development, her line of skyscrapers, they know that America too may claim that her national *motif* is represented, not by the factory or the warehouse, but by the souls of many races touched by that same divine spark, love of freedom.

And this unity has grown in ever-increasing importance as nation after nation has begun to question the soundness of the representation idea. To-day, despite differences, despite contemptuous declarations that our type of government has failed, America and Great Britain still cherish the representative idea, conceiving their common faith in it more important than blood relationship, more important than a common tongue, more important than a common economic interest; for it has given more freedom combined with more justice than any other, or all other types of government.

Chapter III

POLITICAL ALLIANCES AND PEACE AND WAR

Ralph Waldo Emerson described Plato as "a man who could see two sides of a thing," a definition which might stand as the ideal of every historian and of every statesman. The man who sees only one side can never be either an historian or a statesman. The best that he can hope to become is a skilful advocate in the one case, a short-sighted politician in the other.

Most international crises are the products of minds intent upon only one side of a question: and the blood guilt of most wars must rest, in the end, upon leaders who fix their minds upon differences, and refuse to search for unities which would appear if they would but cultivate the Platonic vision.

The history of British-American diplomacy has been pre-eminently the history of the search for a substitute for war: and every British-American crisis, save that of 1812, has eventuated in peace, because the representatives of each nation honestly desired peace, and therefore consented, to some extent at least, to see "two sides of a thing."

In the early years of the Republic the search for British-American unities was largely confined to periods of stress when it was evident that the only alternative was war or the discovery of unities enough to justify a rational adjustment. But in recent years this search has been constant, in normal times as well as in periods of special stress and danger: and, in consequence, the discovery of British-American unities has been of increasing frequency. Indeed, it is perhaps safe to say that more has been accomplished toward making impossible a British-American conflict during the last quarter of a century than in the entire century which preceded it. This is partly due to the fact that America's importance, and potential importance, have been clearly revealed during that period to the hitherto indifferent British mind; partly also to the sounder and broader spirit of American historical teaching, which has enabled the younger generation to understand the changes which have taken place in England through the Parliamentary reforms, and other progressive legislation, and in the British Empire through the extension of representative institutions which has made it a real Commonwealth of Nations. But it is due also to a wider vision, a new understanding, on the part of America, of world problems made pressing by

the possession of widely scattered territorial possessions dating from the Spanish-American war
of 1898.

From the myriad crises, great and small, recorded in the history of British-American relations,
many instances might be cited in which America
has made use of the ancient methods of avoiding
or shortening wars: foreign alliance, diplomatic
negotiations, economic pressure, isolation, agreements to arbitrate. The historians of British-
American diplomacy have examined these methods
in detail, and have drawn from them valuable conclusions, applicable to all nations; but as the
attention of mankind centres more and more
closely upon a later method, a permanent court
of international justice, each must be re-examined;
for the value of history consists in its ability to
look backward and re-interpret the past in view
of the problems of the present. There is profound
wisdom in the statement of the recent interpreter
of Aristotle, Herbert Ernest Cushman, who says:
"The mission of the Athenian State, in the eternity
of things, did not appear until every event in its
history had occurred." Just as the appearance of
things varies according as they are viewed from
the one or the other end of the telescope, so the
meaning of incidents in history varies according

to the location in time of the observer. The mission of each nation in the eternity of things cannot fully appear until the lapse of time, the fading out of prejudices, and the availability of essential evidence have made possible real historical judgments. And even those judgments alter as new facts, often at first apparently unrelated, take definite meaning and interpret the past in terms of the ever new present.

America's one permanent foreign alliance, the Franco-American alliance of 1778, for example, meant one thing in 1778; but by 1793 it had taken on a new meaning, due to events which no man could have foreseen; and it was the lessons learned from the change which caused Washington to draw so clear a distinction between "permanent alliances," which he urged his nation to avoid in future, and "temporary alliances" to which he declared it safe to trust "for extraordinary emergencies." A temporary alliance enables a nation to combine with another, or with other nations, to meet an existing emergency, the nature of which is measurably understood. A permanent alliance binds a nation's will for the exigencies of an unknown future, and may, by the appearance of unexpected changes, commit it to a partisanship contrary to its interests, its ethical judgments, or both combined. From one point of view, every treaty may be regarded as an instrument designed to compel a nation to follow a certain course, after it has ceased to consider that course desirable. For so long as the course is deemed desirable, no treaty compulsion is needed.

Few treaties illustrate these dangers more convincingly than the treaty which involved America in the French alliance. Had it been a temporary alliance, to cease when the American Colonies had established their independence, it would, doubtless, have served as well the purpose of each nation. America would have secured the recognition of her independence; and France would have secured her primary purpose, the weakening of her perennial enemy, England.

But the French alliance attempted to determine the relations between the two nations for an indefinite future, Article XII providing that "in case of a rupture between France and England the reciprocal guarantee...shall have its full force and effect, the moment such war shall break out."

Close upon the completion of the war of the American Revolution, by one of those peaceful revolutions called a change of British ministries, England suddenly passed into the control of men far more sympathetic with America's essential aims than the reactionary Bourbon autocracy, calling itself France, could ever have been; and this change completely altered the picture.

The most powerful of the Whig leaders had been so outspoken in their American sympathies during the war that, a few days before Lord North's fall, George Onslow, speaking in the Prime Minister's defence, taxed them, in open Parliament, with responsibility for American successes. "Why," he said, "have we failed so miserably in this war against America, if not from the support and connivance given to rebellion in this very House?" The answer of the Whigs, in words, was the bold declaration that it is not rebellion to defend the traditional rights of Englishmen. But their answer, in action, was more eloquent. They filled the places of the fallen ministry with Whigs, almost every one of whom, from the Prime Minister, Rockingham, down, had publicly declared that the war against America was unjust and wanton. This meant that the party which had made and conducted the war was not to be allowed to negotiate the peace. That task was confided to the friends of America.

The Rockingham ministry, however, which began those negotiations, while a unit with reference to fundamental American issues, proved an unstable compound, and did not survive to finish the task. It was fatally divided upon the vital issue of Parliamentary reform, and is remarkable for its failure to rise to the clarion note sounded by the younger Pitt, already great by virtue of an inherited glorious name, and soon to be recognized as great also by the divine right of genius and vision.

Lord North's Ministry had fallen on March 20, 1782, and on May 7 Pitt hurled in the faces of the anti-reform members of the Rockingham ministry his thunderbolt, a Bill for reforming Parliament. He declared that the House of Commons was not truly a representative body; representing only: "nominal boroughs, ruined and exterminated towns, noble families, wealthy individuals, and foreign potentates." In this sentence we can see in reincarnation the elder Pitt as he stood in that same place, in January, 1766, demanding the repeal of the Stamp Act.

"I would fain know," he had said, "by whom an American is represented here? Is he represented by any Knight of the Shire?... or will you tell him that he is represented by any representative of a borough? a borough which, perhaps, no man ever saw. That is what is called the rotten part of the Constitution.... The idea of virtual representation of America in this House, is the most contemptible that ever entered into the heart of a man.... If this House suffers the Stamp Act to continue in force, France will gain more by your Colonies than she ever could have done if her arms in the last war had been victorious. I shall never own the justice of taxing America internally until she enjoys the right of representation."

The elder Pitt had carried the repeal of the Stamp Act, but the younger Pitt was overruled. The Bill which he so eloquently defended was beaten, and Parliamentary reform had to wait half a century, although the next Ministry combined the friends of America with the friends of Parliamentary reform.

Rockingham died about two months after the defeat of Pitt's Reform Bill, and Lord Shelburne, also a friend of America and political heir to Lord Chatham, became Prime Minister with Pitt as Chancellor of the Exchequer. To them and to their Cabinet colleagues, therefore, belonged the task of concluding the interrupted peace negotiations with the revolted American Colonies, now *de facto* free and independent states. The treaty was to be completed, as it had been begun, not with British enemies but with British friends.

The American peace delegates had been in-structed to be guided in all negotiations by the wishes of "our good friends the French"; but they soon discover that "our good friends, the French," were secretly conniving with France's other allies, the Spanish, to limit the future of the Republic which they had helped to create. They, therefore, ventured to disregard their instructions and negotiated secretly with England, the French being informed, only after America and England had agreed upon the final terms of peace.

When the negotiations were over, and France had reluctantly and indignantly accepted the terms which America and England had concocted, thereby defeating France's secret intrigues with Spain, David Hartley, one of the British Peace Commissioners, wrote: "It may be that the Americans will never want an ally, but if so, it is still in Great Britain."

When the younger Pitt entered upon his first Premiership in 1784, it should have been clear to every American, as it is clear to-day, that the spirit of Chatham was again moving his country toward the destiny of which he had dreamed when he hurled his Jove-like invectives against a parliamentary system now tottering toward its fall. "Pitt is not a chip off the old block," remarked one admirer, as he watched the youthful statesman, "he *is* the old block."

44

But, despite this great change in England, the eight years following the battle of Yorktown were years of bitter disillusionment for Americans. They were years filled with convincing warnings for all men who face the ever-recurring problems incident to attempts to make sovereign States (boasting absolute equality and thinking in terms of local interests only) work in harness, when no pressing and obvious military danger is forcing them to act together. There is to-day a world conscious of the meaning of such disillusionment. What was needed at that time in America is pre cisely what is needed now throughout the world: a sense of a unity wider than a mere State. She suffered because she refused to see that the whole is greater than any of its parts.

The new efficiency which finally came, however, to the United States, with the Constitution of 1789, was due to the fact that the men who sat behind closed doors in the Convention of 1787 had the vision to see and the courage to discard the localism which had jeopardized the great experiment. Until the American Constitution was approved by the American people and put into operation by popular verdict, all unions of sovereign States had operated only upon the State Governments, and all had failed. This one dared to operate upon the individuals in each of the thirteen States, and it did not fail.

The early months of the history of America as a Federal Republic saw the rise of the first political parties under the Constitution, parties developing chiefly out of domestic problems but concerning themselves increasingly also with questions of foreign relations. When, on March 22, 1790, Thomas Jefferson, recently returned from four years of service as American representative in France, took up his post as Secretary of State in Washington's Cabinet, he was convinced that "the liberty of the whole earth was depending on the issue of the contest" in France, and predisposed to allow the latter to interpret the duties of his nation under the treaties of 1778.

The great silent tide which was carrying England toward parliamentary reform and her new future had scarcely touched his consciousness. To him, England remained the tyrant who had sought to enslave her subjects across the ocean.

Looking around him, he found Alexander Hamilton ensconced in the post of Secretary of the Treasury and solving vast financial problems with the certain touch of genius. He found New York, at that time the temporary capital of the new Republic, still the nest of the Tory, and recalled Washington's declaration of 1777: "If America fall, it will be by the death thrust of the loyalists rather than of the British." After a careful inspection of conditions on Manhattan Island he estimated that one-half of the population of New York City was composed of families which had been persistently loyalist during the Revolution, and still thought with regret of the banished British flag. These facts caused him the greater alarm as he slowly made up his mind that Hamilton, a confessed believer in monarchy, was planning to use the power of the Treasury to establish a government like England's, if not indeed a part of it. He whispered this fear to James Madison, "Father of the Constitution," and then a member of Congress, thus cementing a friendship which lasted as long as he lived.

In his confidential diary, called the *Anas*, Jefferson tells a story illustrative to his mind of Hamilton's pro-British visions, "for the truth of which," says the diary, "I attest the God who made me." Jefferson assembled the four members of Washington's cabinet with John Adams, the Vice-President, at dinner, and the conversation turned upon the British Constitution. Adams ventured to express the view that the British Constitution, if purged of its notorious rotten boroughs

47

and general corruption, would be almost ideal. Hamilton at once declared that such changes would make it unworkable—"As it stands...," he said, "it is the most perfect government which ever existed."

Such views of course heightened the impression that Hamilton and his followers were dangerously pro-British; and from that to un-American was but a step easily compassed by Jefferson's political associates. Furthermore, Hamilton was British born, being a native of Nevis, Leeward Islands, in the West Indies. It mattered not to the logic of insinuation, that Jefferson too was British born, as were Washington, Franklin, Patrick Henry, Samuel Adams, John Adams, Knox, Randolph, and practically every member of Congress, the Senate, the Judiciary and the State Governments. These latter had been born in British territory which had ceased to be British: but Hamilton's birth-place still remained a part of the British Empire. For this unconvincing reason, and because they believed that America's interest lay with England rather than with her ally, France, Hamilton's party, the Federalists, had to shoulder the heavy load of Revolutionary animosities: while Jefferson's belief that France represented the things for which America should stand gave to his

48

dawning party the burden of being considered a French faction, a burden growing ever heavier as the scenes in Paris darkened.

At first, however, foreign questions played only a subordinate part in the formation and consolidation of political parties. The party of Alexander Hamilton was the party of centralization, the party which gloried in its sponsorship of Hamilton's great financial measures: the honest payment of the national debts, the assumption of the State debts, the establishment of a national bank, the imposition of an excise, an increase of tariff duties. The party of Thomas Jefferson, the popular party, was at first negative, representing distrust of all measures tending to centralization, and the determination to prevent Hamilton from working out into permanent institutions his avowed conviction that:

all communities divide themselves into the few and the many. The few are rich and well-born, the other, the mass of the populace.... The people are turbulent and changing; they seldom judge or determine right. Give, therefore, to the first class a distinct, permanent share in the Government. They will check the boisterousness of the second.

Such views, often and boldly reiterated, gave political value to the accusation that Hamilton and

49

his friends were but a Tory faction disguised, seeking to restore the Americans to the arms of Great Britain. To this charge the Federalists retorted that the Democratic-Republicans, the Jeffersonian populace, were only a French faction, glorying in such atrocities as those reported from France, a faction "turbulent, changing," the enemy of all ordered government.

One hundred and fifty years of historical investigation have established the fact that neither was the Federalist party a pro-British faction, nor was the Democratic-Republican party a pro-French faction, though each group identified America's interest with friendship for one or the other of these countries. Each was but attempting to pierce the Stygian darkness which veiled the future, and to divine the road along which America's safety lay.

By the end of Washington's first term the conflicts had grown strangely bitter, and Jefferson and Hamilton "were pitted against one another like two fighting cocks," to use Jefferson's simile. Each had his newspaper, filled with personal attacks upon the other, as savage as though the two leaders did not belong to the same Cabinet. When Washington tried to soothe them, Jefferson replied that Hamilton was seeking to "undermine

50

and demolish the Republic by creating an influence of his department over members of the Legislature," and described his rival as a man whose history "from the moment at which history can stoop to notice him is a tissue of machinations against the liberty of the country which has not only received him, and given him bread, but heaped honours upon his head."

It was during the period of early fierce hatred between these leaders of the dawning political parties that America's second presidential election came: and Jeffersonians united with Hamiltonians in urging Washington to stand for a second election, each being afraid to face the other without the presence of the man who was the friend of both, and above faction. Washington was reluctant to yield. He had suffered cruelly under the personal attacks which bitter partisans had heaped upon him. "I would rather," he declared, "go to my farm, take my spade in my hand and work for my bread than remain where I am." But a sense of duty, to him the sublimest word in the English tongue, held him. He allowed his name to go before the people for re-election, not because of the pleading of eager admirers, but because of the "perplexed and critical posture of our affairs with foreign nations," and was unanimously chosen

President for a second term just at the moment
when the French Revolution began to take the
aggressive attitude toward other nations which
soon changed it from a domestic into a European
conflict.

From the first, a natural sympathy for an ally in
distress had been everywhere apparent in America,
and this sympathy had been strengthened by
certain instances, reported from time to time,
which gratified America's local pride and strengthened her enthusiasm for the French popular movement. The French Revolutionary cry, "Ça ira,"
was borrowed from the sentence with which
Benjamin Franklin had responded to the news of
the horrors of Valley Forge, in 1777. "Ça ira,"
he had declared, "It will all come right in the
end." When in June 1789, the Commons, in the
newly summoned meeting of the Third Estate
at Versailles, had declared themselves a National
Assembly, and had invited the other two Estates
to join with them, it had been upon the advice of
Thomas Jefferson, America's official representative
in Paris, and godfather of the Convention. When
the Bastille fell, Lafayette had sent its key to
Washington, labelled "A trophy of the spoils of
despotism." When, on October 6, 1789, an in-
furiated Parisian mob had battered down the

defences of the king at Versailles, it was Lafayette, adored of Americans, who prevented the execution of the royal family on the spot.

Among the early actions of the new French Republic was the decree of November 15, 1792, which declared:

> The French nation...will consider that people an enemy which refuses or abandons Liberty and Equality, or which desires to preserve its princes and privileged classes;

and on November 19, she offered French aid to all peoples who desired to regain their freedom. With these challenges to the monarchies of the world, the French Revolution became the aggressive champion of a militant Democracy, and took the road which led to Napoleon and the new autocracy.

On January 21 of the next year, six weeks before President Washington's second inauguration, the menace to all monarchies was even more convincingly emphasized; for on that day Louis XVI paid upon the scaffold the penalty of his inheritance. This execution was justly regarded as a threat against all kings, and the monarchies of Europe had no choice but to arm and unite in defence of the existing order. Within a fortnight France had declared war on England and Holland, and the menaced European monarchies were industriously ironing out old differences, and preparing the Grand Coalition for their mutual protection. Europe had begun to display the new unity which soon forced France, as one Revolutionary orator expressed it, to establish "the despotism of Liberty in order to crush the despotism of Kings."

Circumstances had now reached a point at which it was necessary for America to take a definite position before the world. France as an ally, engaged in dethroning her Bourbons, and erecting a Republic, was one thing: but France as an ally, seeking to revolutionize the world by aggressive warfare was something quite different; and the new conditions demanded of America a definition of what her alliance meant. With the beginning of Washington's second term, therefore, the questions of domestic policy which had brought political parties into the field, and had dominated his first term, suddenly and dramatically gave the primacy to foreign questions. The insinuations of pro-British or pro-French sympathies became the chief elements of party warfare: and for over two decades American politics were largely a reflection of European politics, and Jeffersonian Democracy hated Hamiltonian Federalism with a renewed

passion, feeding upon memories of "the days that
tried men's souls," as Tom Paine had called the
American Revolution.

The news that Great Britain had entered the
coalition against France reached Philadelphia, now
America's temporary capital, early in April, and
was at once dispatched to Mt Vernon, whither
Washington had retired for rest, upon the ad-
journment of Congress. Fully conscious of the
temper of the Democratic-Republicans, who had
recently celebrated, with true Gallic fervour, the
news of France's victory over Prussia at Valmy,
and equally aware of the pro-French enthusiasm
of their leader, his Secretary of State, Washington
at once wrote to Jefferson a letter designed to interpret for him his official duties in the premises.

War having already commenced between France
and Great Britain, it behoves the Government of
this Country to use every means in its power to
prevent the citizens thereof from embroiling us
with either of those powers, by endeavouring to
maintain a strict neutrality.

I therefore *require* that you will give the subject
mature consideration, that such measures as shall
be deemed most likely to effect this desirable purpose may be adopted without delay.

This was a hard command for Jefferson, whose
followers, since England had entered the war,

were insisting with even greater vehemence than
before that the French Revolution was the
reincarnation of the American Revolution; a
resemblance which Mr F. S. Oliver, in his eulogy
of Hamilton, declares "visible only to the eye of
faith gazing over 1000 leagues of ocean." History
is now ready to pronounce the resemblance greater
than that: but there was certainly a wide difference
between this frantic movement, blatantly demanding the death of monarchy everywhere, and the
conservative demand of the American Colonies a
few years earlier that they be allowed to keep the
free governments which as British colonists they
had been encouraged to develop.

In an American Cabinet meeting there are many
voices, but one vote, and Washington had already
decided that this vote should go, not for France,
not for the Grand Coalition, but for America,
whose duty he conceived in terms of strict
neutrality.

Probably no single incident in America's diplomatic history has been more frequently censured
than this decision. The world of fair-minded men
has long ago agreed to absolve Washington from
the suspicion of treachery or even of unfair dealing
in this great crisis of his nation's history. But we
must take account also of the never small world

of men who seek to defend a present evil deed by misinterpreting past actions which were entirely justifiable and pointing analogies where none exist. It is therefore important to examine with care the facts with reference to America's obligations to France in this supreme moment.

The Franco-American alliance of 1778 involved two treaties:

1. A treaty of *amity* and *commerce*, acknowledging the independence of the United States, and establishing commercial intercourse.

2. A treaty of *defensive alliance*, stipulating that, should war break out between France and Great Britain *in consequence of France's friendly advances to America*, the two nations, France and the United States, should make common cause against Great Britain; and that neither should make a truce or peace without the consent of the other.

By Article II of the latter Treaty, the alliance was described as *defensive*, and by Article XI the "essential and direct end" of the agreement was declared to be "to maintain effectually the liberty, sovereignty and independence" of the United States, "as well in matters of Government as in Commerce." In return, the United States guaranteed "to His Most Christian Majesty the present possessions of the Crown of France, in America, as well as those which it may acquire by the future treaty of peace." And Article XII expressly stipulated that "in case of a rupture between France and England the reciprocal guarantee declared in the said Article shall have its full force and effect the moment such war shall break out."

Upon the face of the facts it is clearly apparent that the United States was not bound by these treaties to give active aid to France except in so far as the specific guarantees of the treaties promised such active assistance: and France subsequently declared, through her regular diplomatic agents, that she had not desired the United States to enter the war.

This fact was clear to Washington from the first, and it soon became evident that it was equally clear to all the members of his Cabinet, even to Jefferson, ardent enthusiast for France though he was. France was not *defending* herself in a war brought on by her friendship with America, nor was she fighting a *defensive* war. She had herself challenged the established Governments of all monarchies, thus calling the Grand Coalition into the arena by her crusading devotion to her new-born dream of a world of Republics to be erected on the ruins of monarchy everywhere. This fact did not justify the specious contention, subsequently urged by Hamilton, that treaties entered into with the Monarchy need not hold good under the Government which had overthrown the Monarchy. The view of Jefferson, upon this question, will be universally recognized as the only view which can be taken by an honourable nation: These treaties, he declared, were not "between the United States and Louis Capet, but between the two nations of America and France...the nations remaining in existence, though both of them have since changed their forms of Government."

International Law, as Vattel had long ago pointed out, had, even before his day, established the fact that "the State and the nation are always the same, whatever changes are made in the form of government, and the treaty concluded with the nation remains in force as long as the nation exists."

When Washington met his Cabinet, on April 19, 1793, he found unanimous agreement with his conviction that neutrality was the unquestionable right of the United States, but he found a grave difference of opinion among his advisers regarding the method of making public this policy. If the Legislature, Hamilton argued, has the constitutional power to declare war, the Executive has the duty to preserve peace until war is declared.

Therefore the President alone may proclaim neutrality: for that is but a method to preserve peace. Jefferson, on the other hand, opposed the suggestion of a declaration of neutrality by presidential proclamation. To his mind the issues were such as, in free governments, should be left to those whose lives and fortunes must be the hazards in case of a false step which might make war inevitable. He strongly insisted, therefore, that Congress should be assembled in special session and allowed to speak for the people.

Since that memorable contest, the world has travelled along the Jeffersonian rather than the Hamiltonian road; and men have begun to feel that issues of peace and war belong of right to the masses of mankind. But, in this instance, Hamilton won the day, for Washington ultimately agreed with him, as did Knox, "acknowledging," as the *Anas* scornfully records, "...like a fool as he is, that he knew nothing about it." Jefferson, however, carried his point that the word "neutrality" should not be used in the proclamation, but reserved as a prize to be bargained for by the belligerents. The proclamation itself was as cold and colourless as words could make it, warning all Americans not to "violate the laws of nations, with respect to the Powers at war, or any of them."

Kipling, in *Square Toes*, gives a characteristi-
cally life-like glimpse of Washington defending
his refusal to go to war against England at the
demand of France.

"Nevertheless, General," one chimed in, "it
seems you will be compelled to fight England."
At once the General wheeled on him and asked:
"And is there any thing in my past which makes
you think I am averse to fighting Great Britain....
But I know my duty. We must have peace with
England."

And he had peace with England, despite insult,
despite clamour, despite other peoples' reading of
the obligations of the French treaties of 1778.

But, cold as was the attitude of the Government,
there could be no doubt about popular sympathy
for France. In the great cities it expressed itself
feverishly in the form of street demonstrations and
elaborately staged celebrations. And the small
centres reflected the great. In frantic civic feasts,
called to honour France and Liberty, the favourite
decorations were broken crowns, and twisted
sceptres, and the strange terms *Citizen* and *Citess*
swept aside the English terms, Mr and Mrs or
Miss, which smacked of royalty and social grades,
according to the excited American with admiring
eyes on France.

The Federalist newspapers sought to discredit such terms by clever ridicule. One commented that the terms *Citizen* and *Citess* too were undemocratic, suggesting distinctions of sex. Would it not be safer, it asked, to use the general term, *Biped* for all alike? "It is simple, fitted to the people of every country, is both male and female, is not of aristocratic origin, accords with truth, and is free from flattery."

Carried away by their enthusiasm, the unthinking declared neutrality a crime and Washington a usurper and betrayer of friends in distress. Conspicuous among these assailants were Philip Freneau and Benjamin Bache, whose attacks were so furious that, as Washington wrote, "the publications in Freneau's and Bache's papers are outrages on common decency."

In the meantime a new and exasperating element had launched itself into the controversy, in the person of the eccentric youth, still in his twenties, Citizen Edmund Genêt, minister from the French Republic, who had landed at Charleston, South Carolina, on April 8, 1793.

Largely on account of new dramatic elements which he introduced into the picture, Genêt has been magnified into undue importance. He possessed the art of further inflaming an already excited populace: but he possessed little else to entitle him to the conspicuous place to which historians have assigned him. The really important elements in his connection with the grave problems which Washington was so patiently facing, were his instructions and his bad judgment. He had been given secret orders to bring America into the war against England and the Grand Coalition, and, without waiting to present his credentials, he began to work in that direction, treating the nation as though it were his own. With a box full of blank commissions and letters of marque, and a mouthful of phrases of revolution and friendship, he rapidly began turning American citizens into soldiers in the great cause of French, and, by implication, universal liberty. Having made his warlike adjustments to his own satisfaction, erecting courts of admiralty, commissioning privateers, conferring French military titles even upon Red Indians, Citizen Genêt took his spectacular way to Philadelphia, to be received by an indignant President and an indignant Cabinet.

His pathway was thronged by enthusiastic lovers of the new France across the seas: and Genêt accepted their acclaim in fervent addresses, in dramatic renderings of the *Marseillaise*, in liberty-cap ceremonies, and even in the ghastly ceremony of passing around the head of a pig, symbol of royalty, into which each ardent champion of France was granted the aesthetic privilege of plunging a knife, thereby confessing sympathy with the bloody work of the French National Convention.

Public tension against neutrality was by this time so high that crowds, ten thousand strong, assembled in the streets of the national capital, declaring their intention of forcing Washington to resign or declare for France: and in one shameful pageant, called "The Funeral of Washington," the President was placed on the guillotine in parody of Louis XVI.

Genêt reached Philadelphia mad with a sense of power, and with no conception of his real situation till, on May 18, 1793, he stood face to face with the President. But Washington's grim countenance and cold greeting quickly enlightened him and enlightened his admirers as well. The country itself had not fully known Washington till that moment. It had deemed the proclamation of neutrality a party measure, into which the President had been led by those enemies of France, the partisans of England. Now, however, they saw him as he was, saw his majesty of self-control, his awful courtesy and stillness in wrath which ever made him a man to be feared in moments of sharp trial of strength. He accepted, unconditionally, Genêt's credentials of official character: but sternly frowned upon his lawless actions. One by one his unlawful prizes were seized and justice done upon the captors, whose actions Washington had investgated, and the army of the United States was made ready to check any pro-French risings which might result from the activities of the agents whom Genêt had dispatched. These things were done without threats or superfluous conversation. Washington did not need to talk; he was a man of action.

But his enemies talked, talked constantly, talked insultingly: and Genêt, very young, very foolish, judged Americans by their much speaking, and misjudging Washington's influence with the nation which he had made, committed the fatal mistake of threatening to appeal from the President to the people.

As have many more seasoned diplomats in days of grim crises, Genêt misunderstood the character of the people to whose government he was accredited. His threat was taken as an insult to the nation; as indeed, it was. Perceiving this, when too late, Genêt attempted to deny that he had made such a threat; and actually wrote to President

Washington, demanding a statement "that I have never intimated to you an intention of appealing to the people." Three days later he received a curt note from Jefferson pointing out the fact that the State Department was the proper channel through which communications from foreign ministers were received, and clearly intimating that it was deemed of no importance what threats Genêt may or may not have made.

This correspondence was published in the daily press, and Genêt realized that the cause of France in the East was ruined. In the West, however, he still hoped to embroil the United States with Spain, a member of the Grand Coalition, by inciting an American attack upon the Spanish control of the mouth of the Mississippi: "à faire germer les principes de la révolution française dans la Louisiane, dans le Kentucky et dans les autres provinces qui avoisinent les États Unis," as his correspondence phrases the hope.

But here also he failed, failed signally and without one compensating thrill. "Causes unforeseen," so ran the announcement of abandonment, "have put a stop to the march of two thousand brave Kentuckians who were about to go and put an end to the Spanish despotism on the Mississippi, where the Frenchmen and Kentuckians, united

66

under the banner of France, might have made one nation, the happiest in the world, so perfect was their sympathy."

But even before that date, Genêt's public career was ended. His friends, the Girondists, were out of power, and had he returned to France he would doubtless have lost his head—again. Instead he decided to lose his heart: and having married the daughter of Governor Clinton of New York, lived under the latter's protecting wing, a comfortable if not an exciting life until the end, in 1834, when the American papers told again the story of Citizen Genêt and the stormy days of the Grand Coalition.

On December 31, 1793, Jefferson resigned the post of Secretary of State. He had disposed of Citizen Genêt, but the French alliance still remained to trouble his successors; and it ultimately took a war with France, no less real because never formally declared, to release America from its obligations, real, implied, or fancied. On July 7, 1798, it is true, existing treaties with France were declared abrogated: but the First Republic had melted into the First Consulate in its march toward Napoleonic autocracy before France consented, definitely and by treaty, to release America from the only alliance she has ever known.

67   5-2

Foreign alliance had proved no substitute for war; but its lessons had been written deep upon the mind of Washington, and in his Farewell Address he left them as a permanent legacy to the American people.

Chapter IV

NEGOTIATION AS A SUBSTITUTE
FOR WAR

Thomas Marshall, a celebrated Kentucky orator of the last century, in a eulogy of Washington, exclaimed:

> I have heard men say that Washington was not ambitious: but I say that he was the most ambitious mortal that ever breathed. Most men are content to climb the mountain of eternal fame, slowly and with great difficulty. They grasp a crag here and draw themselves up. They grasp a projection there and draw themselves up. But this man, our Washington, when he came to the mountain of eternal fame, marched straight up its side. And when he reached the top, he found there a little platform, just large enough for one, and he proudly perched himself upon it.

Like most fervid oratory, this is history as she is imagined: for few men have given larger service or suffered greater violence of opposition in return for a fame which they never sought than did Washington. If ambition be the willingness to sacrifice personal to public ends, the desire to serve without counting cost or gain, then indeed there is reason to say, with Marshall, that

"Washington was the most ambitious mortal that ever breathed." For the eight initial and critical years of America's federal life he bore the burdens of Chief Executive. In every great crisis his sympathies were on the side opposed to popular clamour. After each great decision he was the objective of vindictive slander and outrageous insult, from a disappointed majority. Yet, in the end, the people understood the issue and agreed that his decision had been right. Can there be a more perfect fulfilment of Burke's prerequisite of statesmanship, that a representative owes to his Constituency his judgment as well as his energy?

In the realm of foreign affairs, Washington's first great decision was, as we have seen, the interpretation of America's duty under the French treaty of alliance of 1778, and his decision, once made, was like the "law of the Medes and Persians which altereth not." In the balance against this decision not to join France in her attack upon European monarchy in general, and making it far more difficult than it would normally have been, were certain old grievances, some real, some imaginary, left as the heritage of the Revolutionary War. In the mopping-up process of 1783, as is usual upon such occasions, many questions had been left vague which should have been settled

70

definitely, while many which the Commissioners had considered settled, continued to create friction, causing Americans to hug closer to their bosoms each Revolutionary tale or tradition which could be employed to turn the minds of a new generation against an old enemy.

In the treaty of peace, for example, England had promised that she would, "with all convenient speed," remove her troops, garrisons and fleet from the United States. But, ten years later, she still garrisoned Detroit, Mackinaw, Fort Erie (Buffalo), Niagara, Oswego, Oswegatchie, Point au Fer and Dutchman's Point, Lord Grenville maintaining that the provision had been intended to secure the Americans against further depredations, and not to entitle them to the restitution of property taken from them in war. As America's federal forces were not sufficient for the proper maintenance of the forts in question, he argued that the treaty necessitated their continued occupation by British troops.

Thus the British troops had remained, and to their evil machinations the Americans ascribed each Indian massacre on the frontier. In some instances Englishmen had led plundering expeditions of savage warriors: in some instances British-made arms were found upon the bodies of

71

slain Indians. As always, in such disputes, there was some truth and much misapprehension upon each side: but available evidence was of course against the British, as there were no British families in lonely cabins to be visited and murdered by American-instigated savages.

On the other hand, Great Britain claimed, with justice, that America had failed to arrange for the legal collection of debts due to British subjects from individual Americans, although the treaty of peace, in Article IV, declared: "It is agreed that creditors on either side, shall meet with no lawful impediment to the recovery of the full value, in sterling money, of all bona fide debts heretofore contracted." The British also complained that the American Government had not stopped the persecution of the Tories at the close of the war: and this accusation too was true, though the additional assertion that she was bound by the treaty to stop such persecution will not bear a reading of the text, since with reference to this subject the American Commissioners had realized that they could make no binding promises. The treaty of 1783 was therefore carefully guarded in the wording of the Tory clause, Article V, which declared:

Congress shall *earnestly recommend* it to the legislatures of the respective States, to provide for the

72

restitution of all estates, rights and properties, which have been confiscated, belonging to real British subjects, and also of the estates, rights, and properties of persons resident in districts in the possession of his Majesty's arms, and who have not borne arms against the said United States. ...and that Congress shall *earnestly recommend* to the several States a reconsideration and revision of all the acts or laws regarding the premises, so as to render the said laws or acts perfectly consistent, not only with justice and equity, but with the spirit of conciliation, which on the return of the blessings of peace should universally prevail. And that Congress shall also *earnestly recommend* to the several States, that the estates, rights and properties of such last mentioned persons, shall be restored to them, they refunding to any persons who may be now in possession, the bona fide price (where any has been given) which such persons may have paid on purchasing any of the said lands, rights or properties, since the confiscation. And it *is agreed*, that all persons who have any interest in the confiscated lands, either by debts, marriage settlements, or otherwise, shall meet with no lawful impediment in the prosecution of their just rights.

These words promise that Congress will *earnestly recommend* these actions to the States. But it must be remembered that, under the Articles of Confederation then in operation, the central government enjoyed little power over the States and less influence, and that Franklin and his fellow-Commissioners had warned the British Commission that too much should not be expected from such a recommendation by Congress, a warning by no means unnecessary as subsequent events soon demonstrated. Congress made the recommendations to the States, which received them with demonstrations of popular indignation, and with renewed persecutions.

In vain wiser leaders, even among the Whig element, protested, pointing out that by persecution they were but building up hostile neighbours on the North. That unwise wrath which outlives wars continued the process until about 3 per cent. of the total American population, some one hundred thousand souls, left the country, to lend their strength to Canada, the Bahamas and Spanish Florida.

The memory of such incidents of course increased the feeling in England that the Americans were still enemies: while the Americans fed their wrath with the argument that money kept from the Tories, and even new confiscations, were but just reprisals for the fact that the British armies had carried away 3000 American slaves at the close of the Revolution, and had never compensated the American owners for their loss, although the treaty explicitly declared: that the forces should be withdrawn "without causing any destruction, or carrying away any negroes or other property of the American inhabitants." These and similar contentions had stood in the way of the fulfilment of the express purpose of the treaty which was the establishment and maintenance of "a firm and perpetual peace between his Britannic Majesty and the said States." It is too often the practice of nations to forget that a treaty is in fact broken by violating the spirit of peace which it enjoins. We quarrel over the question, which has sinned, and in quarrelling commit the very sin which all the clauses were meant to prevent.

It was such facts, together with the obvious impotency of the American nation under the Articles of Confederation, which had caused the failure of John Adams' attempt to negotiate a commercial treaty with Great Britain in 1783, and the outburst of popular enthusiasm which had greeted the French Revolution, and its accentuation when Great Britain joined the Grand Coalition had but increased the tension of British-American relations; while Genêt's reception by the people had been interpreted in England as an indication that America would soon be once more fighting on the side of France.

A mutual effort at conciliation under such conditions would have been the wise course: but instead, both nations, with characteristic Anglo-Saxon obstinacy, paraded the pretence that each cared very little whether the other was hostile or friendly. England, as the great power, flaunted indifference, while the Americans, the new power, went out of their way to demonstrate their hostility, increased in certain sections by questions more immediate than the memory of what had been.

The Western people saw in a possible war with England a chance to attack her ally, Spain, whose control of the mouth of the Mississippi River shut them off from a water-way to the ocean and the great markets of the world. The Eastern states cherished the memory of special wrongs and indignities.

England had always claimed—and continued to claim—that naturalization could not absolve a British-born subject from the duty to fight for his native land; and her insistence upon what Americans called *Impressment* was the logical consequence of her views regarding the permanence of British citizenship. As Laurence points out, in his *Visitation and Search*: "It was never claimed that the officer of a British man-of-war could enter a neutral vessel for the purpose of searching for seamen": but it was claimed that, in strict conformity with International Law, he was at liberty to search all neutral merchant vessels for contraband of war, and that it was no violation of a neutral flag to arrest British subjects when discovered during the process. The Prince Regent, in a declaration issued in January, 1813, thus formulated the British position: "His Royal Highness can never admit, that, in the exercise of the undoubted and hitherto undisputed right of searching neutral merchant vessels, in time of war, the impressment of British seamen, when found therein, can be deemed any violation of a neutral flag."

Indeed, from the British point of view, the wrong was on the other side: for Great Britain was convinced that the new Republic was offering naturalization and the protection of American citizenship as an inducement to desertion from the British navy.

The difficulties incident to these irreconcilable views were heightened by the fact that British-born subjects could not be easily distinguished from American-born citizens of British ancestry, and it therefore frequently happened that, even without malign intent, British ship-captains seized American-born seamen serving upon American vessels,

77

and impressed them into service upon British men-of-war. But it also not infrequently happened, of course, that impressments were made with the determination that British should remain British, whatever America might think about the question of expatriation.

To Americans, however, trained to believe that naturalization carried with it all the rights to protection which birth could give, such distinctions had no weight. They resented alike impressment by mistake and impressment by intent; both were insults to the flag, both were violations of neutral rights, and both should be resisted by a government possessed of due regard to the duty of protecting its nationals.

In addition to these causes of British-American hostility there soon developed a new incentive to war against Great Britain in the revival of the Rule of War of 1756, which declared that a neutral could not enjoy in time of war a trade which had been closed to her in time of peace.

In time of peace, America had been allowed to trade with the French West Indies, but only in vessels so small as to be of little commercial importance. But when France began to feel the pinch of war, caused by the tightening around her of the iron cordon of the British navy, she threw those islands open to American vessels regardless of size, hoping thus to feed her people.

Nothing loath, Americans hastened to take advantage of the larger privileges thus offered them, only to be confronted by the announcement from England that under the rule of 1756, she would consider that all vessels so trading were lawful prizes. Hundreds of American vessels, and hundreds of thousands of American capital, were thus placed in danger of capture.

When Jefferson retired from the Cabinet on December 31, 1793, he left to Madison a recommendation that the United States should discriminate, in tariff regulations, against England, with the purpose of making the latter respect neutral rights. This was the prelude to his later attempt to employ economic pressure as a substitute for war, an attempt which failed so disastrously as to write failure over the whole of the last few years of his second term. Madison presented the plan to the House of Representatives in a set of resolutions, which the Federalists were quick to resent as designed to bring America into the war against Great Britain. At once they consulted their oracle, Alexander Hamilton, still Secretary of the Treasury, who prepared a speech against discrimination which Smith of South Carolina delivered in the House. He solemnly warned the people that the proposed policy would not be a substitution of economic pressure for war, but would lead to war against England on the side of France, the very disaster from which Washington's wise neutrality proclamation had so far saved them. It even ventured to touch the note of fear, painting dramatically the inevitable picture of frontier massacres which must surely follow, forgetting the fact that this note has never harmonized well with the other notes of Anglo-Saxon choruses.

The debate pro and con raged violently, and before its conclusion a new act of ill-will on the part of England came to light. Through her agency, Portugal had let out eight of the Algerine pirate vessels which had been kept penned up in the Mediterranean, and it was generally believed that this had been done with a view to injuring American commerce, as American vessels, being neutral, were accustomed to sail without convoy. It was this action which caused the United States to appropriate money for the construction of six frigates; and thus began the history of the American navy.

War with England now appeared inevitable. Only one chance of avoiding it could be seen. If the President would send a special envoy to England, and this envoy should succeed in persuading her to cease her aggressions and to make a treaty, neutrality might yet be preserved: otherwise war must come.

The question of whom to select for the delicate mission was the subject of much discussion. Madison, Adams, Jefferson and Hamilton were all considered, the latter being the unanimous choice of the most trusted advisers of the President. But pressing domestic duties required Hamilton's presence in the national capital, and accordingly John Jay, Chief Justice of the Supreme Court, was chosen.

In submitting Jay's name to the Senate for confirmation, on April 16, 1794, Washington declared that "peace ought to be pursued with unremitting zeal before the last resort, which has so often been the scourge of nations, is contemplated." By a vote of eighteen to eight, the Senate confirmed the appointment, and on May 12, Jay sailed from New York.

He had scarcely left the harbour when news came that Lord Dorchester, British Governor of Canada, had recently assured the Canadian Indians, in a public address, that there might soon be war between the United States and Great Britain. As Lord Dorchester had but just returned from

England, his remarks were naturally interpreted in America as revealing the present policy of the British Government, and served to inflame further the American war spirit. Documents since revealed prove that Lord Dorchester did not interpret the policy of the Ministry; and they further prove the injustice of the American belief that his speech was meant to incite the Indians to war against the Americans. But the facts as then available caused Washington to inform Congress that this new state of things suggested "the propriety of placing the United States in a posture of effectual preparation for an event which, notwithstanding the endeavours to avert it, may, by circumstances beyond our control, be forced upon us."

In view of such facts, it is evident that Jay's mission was an adventure toward the discovery of unities not at the time apparent, a courageous attempt, in the face of an inflamed war spirit, to substitute rational negotiation for its grim alternative. And John Jay proved the ideal man for the task. Trained as a jurist, a lover of peace, and with a mind singularly free from the pettiness which magnifies differences, he at once saw and reported a disposition on the part of King George III, and of Lord Grenville, his Foreign Secretary, "to give concession a fair experiment by doing us substantial justice, and by consenting to such arrangements favourable to us as the national interests and habitual prejudices would admit." He found, however, that to the British mind fair concessions did not mean that she should allow France to feed her citizens and subjects through the instrumentality of neutral vessels, thus nullifying the advantages which the victories of the British navy had won.

Thus Jay's task, despite the friendly reception which had been given him, was extremely difficult. Indeed, his instructions imposed an impossibility.

1. He must secure the prompt evacuation of the north-western forts.

2. He must secure compensation for the recent seizures of American vessels.

3. He must secure payment for the 3000 slaves which the British troops had carried away, contrary to the provisions of peace.

4. He must try to have the question of the payment of British debts submitted for settlement to American tribunals.

5. He must agree to no treaty which did not open up for the United States trade relations with the West Indies.

6. He must see that his treaty did not contravene any treaty conditions with France.

6-2

Other matters were to be left to Jay's own discretion: but these six requirements were much to expect him to gain from a nation which looked upon America as helpless, and which suspected her of a desire to help France if she dared. Furthermore Jay had to deal with Lord Grenville, one of the ablest diplomats in Europe, and one who had a united nation at his back; while Jay was conscious that whatever he should gain, he would be fiercely attacked by the extreme French and anti-administration party at home.

The negotiations lasted from July 30 to November 19, 1794, and on the latter date Jay signed his name to the completed treaty. The original treaty and a copy were then placed upon separate vessels and sent to Washington at Philadelphia.

While yielding many points which might justly have been insisted upon, Jay had secured agreement upon some new features which have proved of compensating advantage. The treaty made reciprocal provision for the equalization of import and export duties, provided for arbitration as the method of settling certain existing differences between the two nations, declared it "unjust and impolitic that debts...contracted...by individuals having confidence in each other, and in their respective governments, should ever be destroyed

84

or impaired by national authority on account of national differences," provided that there should be no confiscation or sequestration of debts in case of war between the two nations, required each to present causes of complaint before proceeding to war or reprisals, and made provision, limited but of proper tendency, for the extradition of criminals.

In the meanwhile, long before the treaty had reached America, a fierce attack was being planned upon it by the Democratic-Republicans. Every bit of news about it, authentic or otherwise, was eagerly welcomed and used as a pretext for denouncing it in advance. It was reported that Jay had kissed the Queen's hand, on arriving in London, and the French sympathizers in America at once declared: "He has betrayed America with a kiss." "He richly deserves to have his lips blistered to the bone."

Upon this convincing proof of Jay's intended treachery, his enemies prepared an effigy of him, which after numerous suitable ceremonies, was guillotined, after the French fashion of the day. Its clothes were then set on fire and the image blown into fragments by the powder with which it was filled.

On March 7, 1795, the text of the treaty reached Philadelphia; and Washington guarded it with care, determined to master its contents before deciding whether or not to submit it to the Senate for ratification. Obviously Jay had failed to secure most of the concessions which his instructions had demanded: but, on the other hand, the treaty seemed the only alternative to immediate war.

This delay brought upon Washington renewed attacks from the war-wishers. The treaty, they roared, belongs to the people, and the people's representatives are not allowed even to see it. The President seems to regard it as a document affecting him alone.

On June 8, Washington laid the treaty before the Senate, in executive session, asking their "advice and consent," and trusting to the secrecy of executive session to keep it from the public until a decision should be reached.

After brief examination, the Senate discovered that Article XII, by an inexcusable oversight on Jay's part, prohibited the transportation of American cotton in American vessels, and that the treaty failed effectively to open trade with the British West Indies. It therefore required, as a condition of ratification, that an article be added suspending such sections of Article XII as related to trade between the United States and the West Indies. The treaty thus altered was ratified by the Senate on June 24, 1795, subject to Great Britain's acceptance of the alteration, and subject of course to Washington's approval.

Before that approval was given, and despite the most careful provisions against publicity, an opposition Senator, Mason of Virginia, decided that it was his duty to let the people know what the President and the majority of the Senate deemed it wise to withhold. He accordingly sent his confidential copy of the treaty to Benjamin Franklin Bache, editor of the *Aurora*, whose publication Washington had once denounced as an outrage on common decency. Bache prepared excerpts which were published the next day, and on July 1, 1795, further rejoiced the opposition by distributing the entire document, neatly printed in pamphlet form, thus giving them a somewhat more definite reason for their wrath.

As soon as the excerpts appeared, the attacks based hitherto upon guesses as to the probable provisions of the treaty, became frenzied denunciations of unmeasured bitterness. Jefferson declared its negotiation "an infamous act, stamped with avarice and corruption." Bache, with eager pen, but badly mixed metaphor, described it as "an imp of darkness, illegitimately conceived, which, if the Senate expect to cram it down the throats of the people, they mistake their objects."

In Philadelphia, Chief Justice Jay was again paraded in a transparency, bearing in his right hand a pair of scales, with one pan labelled "American Liberty and Independence," and the other marked "British Gold": and the gold side was down. In its left hand the effigy held the treaty, and from its mouth came the insulting inscriptions, "Come up to my price and I will sell you my country."

Popular meetings were held upon every side, and Jay was denounced as a traitor worthy to be guillotined. At Charleston, John Rutledge, whom Washington had appointed Chief Justice to succeed Jay (who in his absence had been elected Governor of New York), declared that Jay was either a fool or a knave, thereby exhibiting so unjudicial a mind that the Senate vetoed his appointment upon the supposition that he must be insane.

With characteristic wisdom, Boston reserved her official denunciations until the arrival of the text. But meanwhile she took occasion, unofficially, to demonstrate the fact that the "Spirit of 1776" still dominated her. Toward the end of June, a British privateer disguised as a French trader and christened "The Betsy of St Croix" had entered Boston harbour, to be promptly recognized by the French Consul as "no Frenchman," and denounced. As the news spread, Boston became once more a city of action. Handbills were scattered broadcast, inviting the public to attend and see the destruction of an impudent British privateer:

This night will be performed at the steps, bottom of Long Wharf, a comedy of Stripping the Bermuda Privateer. Citizens! remember there have been near 300 of our American vessels taken by these Bermudians and have received the most barbarous treatment from these damn'd Pirates!!! Now Americans if you feel the spirit of resentment or revenge kindling in your breasts, let us be united in the cause.

When night came the crowd appeared at the Long Wharf; the vessel was boarded, the captain and crew were sent ashore and the masts were cut down. The hull was then towed toward the shore and burned at the water's edge. This incident shows the state of mind of the people just before the text of Jay's Treaty arrived in Boston.

When it did arrive, on July 10, 1795, 1500 men assembled in Faneuil Hall to consider it, and when the question was put "Do the citizens of this town approve of the treaty?" not a hand was raised in assent. A committee of fifteen was then chosen to draft an address to the President, and they incorporated twenty objections to the treaty, chief among which, though not specifically stated, was objection to any peaceful adjustment whatever.

The news of the action of Boston led other towns to take the same step. Handbills were issued in New York denouncing the treaty and calling upon all good citizens to meet at noon on the next Saturday, in front of Federal Hall, to consider it. Hamilton attended the meeting with Rufus King, intending to defend the treaty, but when he rose to address the crowd, he was greeted with hisses and a shower of stones. With the blood streaming down his face, he called upon the friends of law and order to follow him and withdrew. The meeting then appointed a committee to draft a formal denunciation of the treaty and dispersed.

It now became the favourite amusement of the Democratic-Republicans to insult Jay and the British flag. Some of the anti-treaty toasts at public dinners show the spirit:

1. Clip't wings, lame legs, the pip and an empty crop to all Jays.

2. May this cage made for the American eagle prove a trap for Kingbirds and Jays.

3. May Jay and his treaty "be forever politically damned."

4. May John Jay enjoy all the pleasures of Purgatory.

During all this endless fanaticism and senseless abuse, Jay remained apparently unconcerned. He seemed a disinterested spectator rather than the cause and object of these fierce personal attacks, remarking only: "God governs the universe and we have only to do our duty wisely and leave the issue to him."

Washington too was cool and deliberate in his course. Upon receiving a report that Great Britain had issued new instructions for the seizure of provisions bound for France, he delayed the final action of signing the treaty: but, convinced by investigation that this was untrue, he affixed his name to the document thus making it the law of the land.

At once new insults were showered upon him, unbelievable in their extent and violence. Certain individuals, as Freneau, Bache, and other firebrands of the Press had, in the past, thus offended him, but had lost caste by so doing. Genêt had ventured upon the same course, only to find his ardent followers grown suddenly cold. But, when Washington affixed his name to Jay's treaty, his popularity vanished, and he was denounced, with impunity, in terms, which he himself declared, "could scarcely be applied to a Nero, to a notorious defaulter, or even to a common pickpocket."

In this excited state of the public mind the House of Representatives shared. The treaty was made: the President and the Senate had ratified it: and it had been proclaimed the supreme law, but the Democratic-Republicans' leaders had no idea of accepting it. They knew that, although according to the Constitution they had no part in the treaty-making powers, an appropriation must be made by them before the treaty could become effective. They determined, therefore, to prevent this appropriation, and thus defeat the treaty.

This plan was set in motion by Edward Livingston, who, on March 2, 1796, moved: "That the President of the United States be requested to lay before the House a copy of the instructions to the Minister of the United States who negotiated the Treaty with the King of Great Britain...together with the correspondence and other documents relative to the said treaty." On March 7, when the motion came up for debate, he added the clause, "excepting such papers as any existing negotiation may render improper to disclose."

Although the Democratic-Republican members

disclaimed the view that the House is entitled to a share in making treaties, they obviously intended, in this instance, to employ their control of the purse to defeat a treaty which would in effect give them always the final voice; and by a vote of sixty-two to thirty-seven they passed Livingston's resolution.

Washington's cautious reply was a promise to give their demand his careful consideration; which careful consideration deepened his first conviction that the demand should be refused. Accordingly, on March 30, 1796, he sent to the House of Representatives a carefully written message, positively refusing their demand and presenting his reasons.

"The power of making treaties," he said, "is exclusively vested in the President, by and with the advice and consent of the Senate, provided two-thirds of the Senators present concur....Until now, without controverting the obligation of such treaties, they (the House of Representatives) have made all the requisite provisions for carrying them into effect....As therefore it is perfectly clear to my understanding that the assent of the House of Representatives is not necessary to the validity of a treaty; as the treaty with Great Britain exhibits in itself all the objects requiring legislative provision, and on these the papers called for can throw no light,...a just regard to the Constitution and

93

to the duty of my office...forbids a compliance with your request."

The House next turned its attention to the question: Shall the appropriation necessary for carrying Jay's treaty into-effect be made by the people's representatives? Of the debate which followed, John Marshall, "the Great Chief Justice," later wrote: "Never has a greater display been made of argument, of eloquence and of passion." James Madison led the fight against the appropriation. He catalogued the people's objections to the treaty as though it were still pending. He demonstrated the fact that Jay had almost completely failed to secure the specific concessions enumerated in his instructions. He proved conclusively that by the treaty France was forbidden practices which were allowed to England.

In the Senate, while the treaty was pending, his argument would have been in order; but in the House of Representatives, with the treaty already ratified and binding upon the nation, it was singularly inappropriate, especially as the plea of a man whom history has christened "the Father of the Constitution." Madison, of all living men, should have acknowledged the fact that a treaty, when ratified by the President and the Senate, is a pledge of honour, already given.

Many men who listened to that debate could see the fallacy in such argument: but it was convincingly exposed by only one. Fisher Ames, a Representative from Massachusetts, was a man clearly marked for an early grave. Dying of tuberculosis, and under strict orders from his physicians to take no part in the debate, he had entered the House unprepared to speak: but, as he saw the danger that a treaty, already ratified, might fail, he determined to intervene and plead the binding character of the agreement. As he rose in his place, he was compelled to lean on his desk for support. His physical condition at once commanded sympathy, but his burning sentences soon fixed attention upon his theme, the national disgrace of abandoning a treaty which was already a pledge of honour given by the nation. He showed the war which must result in case of its abandonment, and for which the House would rightly be held responsible. "No Member," he said, "but will think his chance to be a witness of the consequences greater than mine: yet, if the vote of rejection should pass, I, slender and almost broken as my life is, may outlive the government and the constitution of my country."

When Ames ceased speaking, a recess was taken lest the members should vote against their sober consciences under the spell of his eloquence. But when, after the recess, the final vote came, it was 51 to 48 in favour of the necessary appropriation.

And so at last, under conditions as unfavourable as could well be imagined, Great Britain and the United States saw rational negotiation substituted for war, thus entitling all future generations to believe that, between them at least, reason may always triumph.

When we think of Jay's treaty merely from the point of view of the immediate, apparent interests of one nation alone, the United States of America, it is easy to understand the opposition which it met, in the Senate, in the House of Representatives, and before the public, from pulpit, press and platform. But when we think of it, as we should think of all treaties, from the point of view of the growth of a consciousness of international unities, we must see in it a milestone of progress. From the standpoint of that small thing which men call personal ambition, it was for Jay a cancelled passport: but it has served, better than any other act of his life, to give him access to the larger fame which of right belongs to all statesmen with the vision to perceive and the courage to declare the larger vision. And courage, if we may accept the definition of Plato, "is nothing else than knowledge."

Chapter V

ECONOMIC PRESSURE AS A
SUBSTITUTE FOR WAR

When a physician approaches a bedside, his first problem is diagnosis, the definition of the disease which he is called upon to treat. That settled, he brings to bear upon it the collected experiences of past generations of physicians who have met the disease, in one form or another, and have left a record of how they treated it, and of the results.

When a lawyer agrees to act for a client, his first concern is to discover the point of law involved in the case. He then reviews past decisions to see how that point has fared at the hands of the judges of the past, knowing that there is a continuity which will vitally affect his case, although its incidents are different from those of all earlier cases. In like manner, every real statesman employs the experiences of past generations to make easier the solution of his own problems.

Thus all educated life is a long series of argument from analogy, the supposition being always that while the incidents of life are as varied as the dreams of human happiness, the essential principles which constitute life's framework are changeless and eternal.

It is sometimes said that analogies are more often misleading than helpful; but if that were true, the best guessers about the future, in whatever line, would be those with the least knowledge of the past. The best physician would be he who refused to study prior cases and reason from them to his present case; the best lawyer would be he who never turned a page of precedent, nor pondered over the intricate paragraphs of decisions, past and gone, but embalming legal principles perennial in their vitality. The best financial expert would be the *a priori* reasoner with no knowledge of the history of currency, and the development of banking.

The practical value of history lies in the fact that it is the storehouse of previous decisions, not for the lawyer alone, but for every man who seeks to serve his generation by enabling it to profit by the errors and the successes of the past, in Science, in Art, in Religion, in Politics; in all the myriad fields which true history envisages.

But the value of that storehouse of precedents depends upon the method of its use. The ancient Egyptian physician had precedents as have the physicians of our own generation, but the Egyptian law made them his master, not his servant. An Egyptian physician who ventured to treat a case in any manner save as the custom of the past prescribed was liable for murder if his patient died. Our generation is wiser, declaring that the past may instruct but must not master us, that we study the past, not for the sake of the past, but to throw light upon the problems of the present and of the future. The value of history as a storehouse of precedents depends also upon its freedom from special pleading. Lucian wrote, seventeen centuries ago:

A writer of History ought in his writings to be a foreigner, without a country, living under his own law only, subject to no king, nor caring what any man will like, or dislike, but laying out the matter as it is.

The historian who goes beyond that, ceases to be an historian, and degenerates into a mere advocate. As an historian, he is a crusader for one cause only—unbiassed Truth—whether its flaming sword turns toward his own nation or some other. The moment he sways, either to attack or to defend, he ceases to be an historian.

With these restrictions consciously assumed, we approach the great experiment of Thomas Jefferson, the substitution of economic pressure for war.

The circumstances were extraordinary, so extraordinary that we shall doubtless never see them repeated, even approximately, although the grim days of 1914–1917 were strangely similar.

Napoleon Bonaparte, "the man of destiny" as he modestly considered himself, had started his career as a crusader for democracy, a modern Sir Galahad with eyes only for the Sacred Chalice inscribed Human Liberty. In this name he had assumed leadership in a madly liberated France, dedicated, Don Quixote like, to the task of tearing down every throne in Christendom, and with a genius which no one has ever questioned had sought this Holy Graal, until there came to him a more enticing vision, a throne which should cast its shadow across the world. In the path of this ambition, newly conceived and ardently followed, stood Great Britain, perennial enemy of France, whether as a monarchy or as a crusading republic; and no less the enemy of Napoleon's new dream of a world empire.

For a time it seemed likely that the United States too would recognize in Napoleon an enemy: for on October 1, 1800, he took from Spain the American province of Louisiana, nominally by purchase but really by virtue of his personal power. The holder of Louisiana controlled the

Mississippi River through which alone the products of America's vast western territory could reach the sea. Thus the shadow of Napoleon's rising throne fell across the American Continent, and President Jefferson, after some months of pondering, wrote the startling words:

The day France takes possession of New Orleans fixes the sentence....From that moment we must marry ourselves to the British fleet and nation... and prepare for holding the two continents of America in sequestration for the common purposes of the United British and American nations.

It is interesting to speculate what doctrine would have stepped in before the Monroe doctrine had France taken possession of New Orleans, and had Jefferson solemnized the marriage. History, however, deals, not with speculation, but with fact. Napoleon did not take possession of New Orleans, and Great Britain was the cause. The younger Pitt, at the critical moment, foreseeing the end of the peace of Amiens, and conscious, as he had recently remarked, that the Corsican was still "the same rapacious, insatiable plunderer," rose from the dead, politically, and prepared England for a renewal of war with France.

There was power in "the Pilot that weathered the storm," as his followers later called him: and

Napoleon recognized that power even before the testing time. Therefore, when, in January 1803, James Monroe was sent to Paris to secure a free navigation of the Mississippi by the purchase of the island of New Orleans, he found a very responsive Napoleon ready to sell not New Orleans only, but the whole Louisiana province. "It is certainly worth while," he remarked, "to sell when you can what you are certain to lose...for the English...are aching for a chance to capture it." When his two brothers, Lucien and Joseph, objected to the sale, declaring it unconstitutional, Napoleon replied: "We are past that, you had better believe...I shall do just as I please," and so he did, mockingly calling the action 'Louisianicide.'

On April 30, 1803, a treaty of purchase and two conventions regarding Louisiana were accepted by Napoleon, and early in May they were signed. It was not too soon. In mid-May, Pitt appeared in the House, like a stormy petrel presaging a tempest. "Never," wrote an eye-witness, "...was there such an exhibition....He spoke nearly two hours, all for war, and war without end." Fox, conscious of the greatness of the outburst, its elevation of thought, its eloquence of diction, its masterfulness, declared that if Demosthenes had been present he might have been envious.

With the clairvoyance which combined with the other elements of his genius to make him the world's greatest menace, Napoleon had foreseen that England would take this course, and by selling Louisiana to the United States had planned, as he remarked, to give England "a rival who sooner or later will humble her pride."

Thus it is evident that, while America owes the possession of the vast Louisiana purchase to the initiative of Napoleon, she owes him no gratitude for the action. King John gave Magna Carta to the world: but the world's gratitude belongs rather to the gallant barons who forced the despot's hand.

The facts seem to justify the belief that Napoleon, when he made the Louisiana cession, resembled King John in another respect; he did not intend the concession to be final. In both cases the act was an act of expediency designed to be as temporary as circumstances would permit. King John did not abandon his dream of autocratic government, and Napoleon, when he sold France's imperial domain across the sea, probably had no intention of permanently relinquishing the age-long French dream of an American Empire. He had put Louisiana into safe neutral hands until his vision of a conquered Europe should be fulfilled:

and when Barbé-Marbois, the French negotiator of the treaty of cession, pointed out that the boundaries of the pawned province were uncertain, Napoleon replied: "If an obscurity did not already exist, it would perhaps be good policy to put one into the treaty" [see Appendix].

The acquisition of Louisiana settled the old contest over the navigation of the Mississippi, a contest which had often threatened to eventuate in war, and Jefferson's vision of a marriage with the "British fleet and nation" which the news of Napoleon as a near neighbour had called forth, vanished into air.

Left free to devote his energies to domestic problems, Jefferson was soon deep in plans for destroying the little navy which Washington had started in the menacing days before Jay's treaty made peace with England. His idea of national defence centred upon a fleet of four light-draft vessels of sixteen guns each for foreign service, and fifteen three thousand dollar gunboats for defence of American rights on the Mississippi, which latter, he declared, would require only one gang of plunderers to look after them. In 1804 two of these gunboats were built and launched. No. 1 was struck by a Georgia cyclone and driven ashore where she was left securely planted in a cornfield, where, laughed the Federalist, she may grow into a ship-of-the-line before war comes again. Another humorist suggested that she there rendered her best possible service—as a scarecrow, and Rufus King, Minister to Great Britain from 1796 to 1803, answered to the toast:

If our gunboats are of no use upon the water, may they...be the best upon earth.

Obviously the President was looking for some method of protection less expensive than armies and navies; and the election of 1804 placed the seal of popular approval upon his search. He was re-elected President by a majority so convincing that his carping critics captured only fourteen electoral votes.

On December 2, 1804, barely a month after Jefferson's re-election, Napoleon crowned himself Emperor of France, and began his self-imposed task of making the kingdoms of Europe dependencies of his Empire. But so little did the Sage of Monticello understand the meaning of that event that, in his second Inaugural Address, he did not mention the great Corsican but dismissed foreign affairs with the doctrine, doubtful when one faces a Napoleon, that "a just nation is trusted on its word, when recourse is had to armaments and wars to bridle others."

Perhaps this idealistic view might have proved nearer the truth had not America's neutral position proved so profitable, so well-nigh unbelievably profitable. American foreign tonnage by 1805 was almost a million, and her vessels carried nine-tenths of America's export and import trade, aggregating over $150,000,000. This vast increase was of course due to disturbed conditions in Europe, and was made at the expense of British and French carrying trade. "With the exception only of a very small portion of the coasting trade of our enemies," wrote J. Stephens in an illuminating book called *War in Disguise*, "not a merchant sail of any description now enters or clears from their ports in any part of the globe, but under neutral colours."

When the year 1805 opened, this vast trade seemed safe, conforming as it did to British law as interpreted by Sir William Scott, of the Admiralty Court, in the case of *The Polly* (1800). It was highly acceptable to Napoleon, and England had not yet taken official notice of the fact that America was breaking the continuity of the voyages with no intention of observing the obvious intent of the British Navigation Acts; keeping the word of the decision, to break down its spirit. In other words they were enjoying in time of war a trade closed to them in time of peace, thus feeding the armies with which Napoleon was hoping to conquer the world.

In the summer of 1805, however, Sir William Grant, of the British Court of Appeal, a tribunal higher than the Admiralty Court, condemned the American vessel, the *Essex*, which had conformed to the letter of Sir William Scott's decision, by breaking her journey at Salem and paying the legal duties, only to receive back the money as drawbacks, and proceed to her true destination, Havana. The Court of Appeal decided that the cargo was forfeit as an actual violation of the intention of the British Navigation Acts and of the Rule of War of 1756, which decision, as about 50 per cent. of America's neutral trade was of a character similar to that of the *Essex*, meant seizures and condemnations on a gigantic scale.

The *Essex* decision was sound from the point of view of Great Britain's traditional policy of insisting upon the Rule of 1756; but from the point of view of America, which held the Rule of 1756 unjust and oppressive, it was supremely unsound. When two nations, in the absence of any power competent to interpret International Law authoritatively for both, sharply disagree upon the acceptance of such law, the question becomes one either of open war or of war in disguise.

The indignant American merchants interpreted the seizures under the *Essex* decision as war, while the British merchants considered America's actions in practical disregard of the Rule of 1756 as giving aid and comfort to Napoleon, for a consideration. Each party, from the point of view of what she considered law, was right; and, perforce, the officials of each nation took the point of view of their own nation.

Thus William Pitt, traditional and hereditary friend of America, son of the great Chatham whose eloquent voice had so often defended America, sustained the *Essex* decision, with its implications, while Thomas Jefferson, author of the recent suggestion to "marry ourselves to the British fleet and nation" set himself the task of defeating the purpose of that decision by the skilful use of economic pressure.

But while Jefferson was musing, the fire burned. On October 21, England gained supreme control over the ocean by Lord Nelson's victory at Trafalgar, and the destruction of the combined fleets of France and Spain. Even this victory, however, did not satisfy American traders that their 'rights' were no longer protectable, though it confirmed the British mind in the belief that it was entitled to disregard them.

In the meanwhile American merchants continued to defy the laws which their nation had neither made nor acknowledged as binding. Gains from the menaced neutral trade were so large as to encourage large risks, and American vessels continued the proscribed trade with such success that, on May 16, 1806, almost four months after Pitt's death, Grenville, the new Prime Minister, felt it necessary to announce what was known as "Fox's blockade," which declared the entire European coast, from the Elbe's mouth to Brest, closed to neutral commerce, a blockade, largely 'paper.'

Against this triad of injustices, as the American people considered them, the Rule of 1756, 'paper' blockade and impressment, what recourse had President Jefferson? Clearly war; but war obviously would insure, temporarily at least, the destruction of the very trade which he was asked to protect. Alliance? That was manifestly an unpromising alternative, since both belligerents were disregarding the rights of the monopolizer of neutral carrying trade, and alliance was but another name for taking sides in the conflict. Negotiation? Negotiation was already being tried, as it had been tried from the first, but with results which approached the absolute zero. Monroe and Pinckney were patiently negotiating with Charles James

Fox, Grenville's Foreign Secretary, and were already convinced that Great Britain desired to avoid injustice even in the matter of impressment, the British representatives having gone so far as to suggest the passage of laws which should make it a penal offence both for British commanders to impress American citizens, and for officers of the United States to grant certificates of American citizenship to British subjects.

But while this fact made it evident that the heart of the controversy lay not in a desire to oppress, it was equally evident that English and American views upon naturalization were irreconcilable. On this subject each side was adamant, and in consequence, despite the desire of each to see justice done, the negotiations were already foredoomed to failure.

In the midst of this discussion came the news that, on October 14, 1806, Napoleon had defeated the Prussians at Jena, and thirteen days later had entered Berlin in triumph. Within a month the Berlin decree of November 21, 1806, had declared the entire British coast closed by a French 'paper' blockade. The British negotiators at once insisted that America promise resistance to the French decree, a demand made the more insistent by the added fact that Napoleon had closed to

British trade all ports under French control, which soon included all of Continental Europe, save Norway, Sweden and Turkey.

It was the cry of Pharaoh modernized, England has "chastised you with whips but I will chastise you with scorpions."

In the end the British too used scorpions, insisting that a note be attached to the pending treaty declaring that, should the United States fail to resist the Berlin decree, England would thereby acquire the right to retaliate, a statement prophetic of drastic action soon to follow in the shape of Orders in Council. The fate of neutral trade appeared sealed; since to trade with one belligerent would render American vessels liable to seizure by the other. Americans might theorize as they pleased about the justice of their views concerning neutral rights: but England had closed the Continent to neutral trade, and Napoleon had closed England. Neutral vessels disregarding either prohibition were treated equally by the belligerents as lawful prizes.

Under these impossible conditions, Monroe and Pinckney completed their negotiations with Great Britain, and President Jefferson shortly held in his hand the treaty which resulted. The British Commissioners had conceded to American vessels the right, denied to them by the *Essex* decision, of carrying European goods, not contraband of war, to any belligerent colony, not blockaded by British ships, under condition that such goods had been actually landed in the United States and had paid a duty of at least one per cent. above any refund made upon re-exportation. They had further conceded that American vessels might carry to European belligerent ports, not under blockade, the products of belligerent colonies, in case those products had been first brought into the United States, and there paid a duty of two per cent in excess of any drawbacks, provided of course that such products were not contraband of war.

But despite concessions, to Jefferson's mind the proposed treaty had one fatal defect. It seemed to him to indicate acquiescence in the British view of impressment. He therefore rejected it without even submitting it to the Senate. The action of course drew upon him bitter criticism, both in England and in America, and in his annual message of October 1807, he thus defended it:

"Some of the articles," he said, "might have been admitted on a principle of compromise, but others were too highly disadvantageous; and no sufficient provision was made against the principal source of the contentions and collisions which were constantly endangering the peace of the two nations."

Alliances and negotiations being thus clearly out of the question, and war being a consideration which he refused to entertain, Jefferson now resolved to test economic pressure, being old enough to remember the days of the Stamp Act and the Townshend Acts, and how economic pressure had forced the mother country to much-desired concessions. Here was his instrument, his substitute for the war, which both belligerents had so defiantly courted.

In the excitement aroused by the British declaration, that the Rule of 1756 would be enforced, Congress had passed a law forbidding importations from the British Empire, but Jefferson had not enforced the law. He now proposed that Congress pass a stronger measure, an absolute embargo for an indefinite period: and on December 22, 1807, he found such a law on his desk ready for Executive approval. At once he signed it, its chief provision being: "that an Embargo...is laid on all ships and vessels in the ports and places within the limits of jurisdiction of the United States...bound to any foreign port or place."

Hitherto embargoes had been for limited periods as preparations for expected declarations of war. But this embargo was different. It was itself the only war contemplated: it was for an indefinite future, and was aimed alike at both belligerents.

Napoleon was quick to see that under this law no American trading vessel had a right anywhere save in American ports, every registered American vessel having been required to "give bond...in a sum of double the value of the vessel and cargo, that the said goods...shall be relanded in some part of the United States." By his Bayonne decree of April 17, 1808, therefore, he directed the capture of all vessels calling themselves American, thus generously aiding Jefferson to enforce his embargo.

It soon became evident that neither France nor Great Britain was likely to yield to warfare by economic pressure, and that America herself was to be the chief sufferer. Whoever else was injured, or escaped injury, American merchants were certain losers, unless, tempted beyond resistance, they ventured to disregard their own law, and trade with Europe, which they freely did. Coasting vessels, clearing for American ports, tried every means of avoiding the bond, and if successful, carried their goods to the foreign ports where they commanded the best prices, regardless of the law. Freights were so high that the temptation to sneak to sea was enormous: and traders on the Canadian frontier devised many ingenious methods of smuggling, from night running to the device of dragging barrels of goods to the top of declivities on the boundary and allowing them to run of their own motion into Canadian territory.

Jefferson's last six months in office were months of hopeless disillusionment. Each day brought his substitute for war into more open contempt. Madison and Gallatin rallied Congress to his aid and secured the passage of the Enforcement Act of 1808, raising the bond to six times the value of the vessel concerned, as arbitrary and inquisitorial a law as the alien and seditious laws which Jefferson had himself denounced as tyranny. A year earlier he would have scorned such instruments: but now he took refuge in the fact that Madison was President-elect, and described himself as "an unmeddling listener."

But Jefferson was still firm upon two points: he would not fight, and he would not permit expenditure for munitions of war, despite the British and French disregard of neutral rights, and despite the practice of impressment.

Washington had trusted to the force of neutrality, but with the precaution which he had commended to his successors in the words: "taking care to keep ourselves, by suitable

establishments, on a respectable defensive posture,"
and he had succeeded. Jefferson had trusted to
neutrality, defended by economic pressure alone,
and he had miserably failed.

Nor was Jefferson's futile policy of defence
allowed to die with the end of his term of office.
As early as February 1809, it was known that the
President-elect, Madison, favoured its repeal: and
Congress acted without awaiting his inauguration.
Three days before the end of Jefferson's term of
office, the embargo was repealed, and on March 4
a new experiment, called the Non-intercourse
Act, began to operate. This Act authorized the
President, should either France or Great Britain
cease to violate neutral commerce, to maintain
non-intercourse with the other nation not ceasing:
but pending such a change he was to maintain
non-intercourse with both.

On that same 4th of March, 1809, President
Jefferson retired to private life, discredited. He
had leaned on a broken reed, and humiliation was
the result. He bitterly resented, while unable to
deny, the caustic summary of John Randolph:
"Never has there been an administration which
went out of office and left the nation in a state so
deplorable and calamitous."

It was unfair then; it would be more unfair now,

to allow Jefferson to bear all of the blame for that colossal failure. The old cry of the fast-receding days of autocracy was: "The king can do no wrong." But the new cry was already, "All wrong is the fault of the President." Then, and even more to-day, the American Executive has to bear the burden of many sins not particularly his own. Is there a drouth or deluge, fire, pestilence or famine, just before an election? an eloquent opposition places the blame on the President's shoulders. Is there a lean year? is there a foreign war to cut down the gains of merchants? is there a panic in Wall Street? we hear the cry, "Away with him!"

For the plan that failed, economic pressure as a substitute for war, the American people, through their chosen representatives, were as responsible as was the President. The policy of withdrawing into the shell, by stopping all shipping, called the "terrapin policy," had been suggested six months before Jefferson entered on his first term as President. The entire Cabinet had approved it; and both Houses of Congress had given it large majorities. It had therefore not failed for lack of governmental support. It had failed because it demanded of humanity more than humanity had shown itself willing to give. If the people of America had sustained the policy, despite the personal losses involved, there seems little reason to doubt that the belligerent nations would have dipped their proud banners in return for food: but all the autocratic machinery of Gallatin's Enforcement Act had failed to keep America's traders from the sea.

Nor was it America alone who could not wield this great two-edged sword—economic pressure. The temptations of high gains had broken down the ordinary standards of commercial honesty and patriotic self-sacrifice in all lands with traders ready for the sea. Napoleon gave licences even to British vessels with which they carried supplies to his needy troops beyond the lines of England's long 'paper' blockade; while American trading permits, forged for the purpose of escaping America's laws, and bogus British papers of privilege were openly sold in London.

In theory, economic pressure was in full operation: in practice, the wicked flourished like the green bay tree, despite law, despite patriotism, even despite constant captures by the belligerent powers, whose laws were being flouted, not alone by enemies and neutrals, but even by their own nationals bent on abnormal gains.

This failure does not prove that a similar method under different conditions and backed by more compelling motives cannot succeed. One swallow does not make a spring, but centuries of record have convinced mankind that at least it justifies the hope that spring will not be long delayed. The fallacy of incomplete induction is a real fallacy: but its use establishes no presupposition that the converse proposition is true. Economic pressure as a substitute for war may yet succeed, under the conditions laid down in Article 16 of the Covenant of the League of Nations which declares:

Should any Member of the League resort to war in disregard of its covenants under Articles 12, 13 and 15, it shall *ipso facto* be deemed to have committed an act of war against all other members of the League, which hereby undertake immediately to subject it to the severance of all trade or financial relations, the prohibition of all intercourse between their nationals and the nationals of the covenant-breaking State, and the prevention of all financial, commercial or personal intercourse between the nationals of the covenant-breaking State and the nationals of any other State whether a member of the League or not.

Soon after taking the oath of office as President, Jefferson's successor, James Madison, was encouraged to believe that the intolerable situation in which America found herself was nearing its end, for on April 18, 1809, the British Minister, David Montagu Erskine, consented to the conclusion of a treaty withdrawing the British Orders in Council of 1807, and the following day Madison joyfully proclaimed the renewal of trade with the British Empire.

At once American vessels swarmed to sea, without waiting for the 10th of June, which date the President had set for the reopening of British trade. They did not know, nor did the President know, that Erskine had been instructed to secure certain American concessions which his treaty failed to secure. This they learned promptly, however, for Canning, now Foreign Secretary, promptly disavowed the treaty and recalled Erskine, thus forcing Madison to restore non-intercourse with Great Britain.

Had not Canning wisely exempted from seizure such American vessels as had sailed trusting to the treaty, it would have been difficult to prevent immediate war. And the insulting innuendoes of Erskine's successor, Francis J. Jackson, and his declaration that Madison had deceived Erskine, and decoyed him into an indiscretion, did not make easier the pathway of peace.

But the pathway of peace was nearing its end. Economic pressure as a substitute for war, in the forms of embargo and non-intercourse had failed, and on May 1, 1810, Congress ventured upon one last method, which history calls Macon Bill No. 2. It threw the seas open to American vessels, and invited all the world to the enjoyment of American trade until March 3, 1811. But, in case either England or France should, before that date, cease to hinder American commerce, the other was to be given three months in which to take a similar step. Should she fail to do so, non-intercourse was to be revived against her alone.

Here was an opportunity for Napoleonic strategy which was not overlooked. By lying pledges, comporting ill with his uninterrupted practices against American commerce, Napoleon induced President Madison to renew non-intercourse against Great Britain alone. Accordingly, on November 2, 1810, in a Presidential Proclamation, Madison recorded bad history and worse policy. Trusting to Napoleon's statement, he declared that the French decrees had been revoked. This meant that unless the British Orders should be repealed before February 2, 1811, non-intercourse would be revived against Great Britain alone.

In vain did the Marquis of Wellesley, then British Foreign Secretary, warn the American Minister in London that Napoleon's promises were lies. Madison believed the lies, and when February 2 came and went, he advised Congress to revive non-intercourse with Great Britain. This Congress did a month later by a large majority.

This decision, aided by the policy of the 'war-hawks,' Clay, Calhoun, and other rising statesmen, soon merged the substitute for war into war itself, which, by the irony of fate, was declared against Great Britain two days after Parliament had definitely repealed the obnoxious Orders in Council.

The war of 1812 was not caused by the Jeffersonian substitute for war: but neither was it prevented by that substitute. And as we look back over the records, we cannot help wondering whether, without that losing experiment, America might not at least have landed on the right side when at last she took up the sword. She did not fight as Napoleon's ally: but she stood as his co-worker. Napoleon was America's true enemy, as we see the facts to-day: for he was the enemy of the institutions which have been her glory from the beginning. From his success America had nothing to gain; all things to lose: while the losses which he had already caused her were far greater than those which she had suffered from Great Britain.

In July 1812, President Madison sent to Congress a tabulated list of losses for the five years ending with the declaration of war against Great

Britain, which list shows 558 vessels taken by the French as compared with 389 taken by the British. And to balance the 389, we have the fact that England was a major factor in the victories which induced the Man of Destiny to settle on the Isle of Elba, a mock-monarch, with an allowance of 800 soldiers at his command, two million francs annuity in his hands and, in his heart, the old, old dream, an empire in America, a dream which had haunted all French rulers since La Salle's descent of the Mississippi in 1682.

Ten months later when, at the end of the War of 1812, the American Senate consented to the Treaty of Ghent, there was small need to quarrel over the question of the right of search or impressment. The fall of the world's enemy had rendered those fiery differences so innocuous, that they were not even mentioned in the treaty of peace. And neither impressment, right of search nor the question of the blockades ever again became serious in the sense of earlier days.

Napoleon, and not permanently irreconcilable views upon the Rule of 1756, 'paper' blockades and impressment, caused the war of 1812. It was his conscienceless skill which caused American citizens to fight, though indirectly, for a cause that was never their cause: and the whole trend of British-

American relations since the treaty of Ghent has served to emphasize the fact that it was not their cause. That American interests were safe with Great Britain victorious over Napoleon was convincingly demonstrated as soon as Napoleon was removed from the stage.

Scarcely had the treaty of Ghent been signed when England's attention was directed toward the south of France, where Napoleon was landing at Cannes, March 1, 1815, to take control of the fickle French populace, and try again the fortunes of his genius in "The Hundred Days."

America had done what she could, without alliance or partisanship with France, to make his vision real: and she did not realize for years after his second downfall, that Waterloo was her salvation, not less than that of Europe. Had Napoleon defeated Wellington, America's recent treaty of purchase of Louisiana would doubtless have become a scrap of paper, a pawnbroker's ticket used by the world's greatest robber to conceal his treasure until the time should come for him to reclaim it.

Beaten, he planned at first a flight to America; but England spoke the word, 'St Helena,' and the career of the Man of Destiny was at an end.

The lessons of the failure to compel peace by

economic pressure were not lost on the keen mind of Madison, whose message of December 5, 1815, has this to say:

Notwithstanding the security for future repose which the United States ought to find in their love of peace, and their constant respect for the rights of other nations, the character of the times particularly inculcates the lesson that, whether to prevent or repel danger, we ought not to be un-prepared for it. This consideration will sufficiently recommend to Congress a liberal provision for the immediate extension and gradual completion of the works of defence, both fixed and floating.

The immediate trend of British opinion after the Treaty of Ghent was in the same direction. The London *Times*, in 1817, declared: "The first war with England made them (the United States) independent: their second made them formidable." But already, as we can now see from the study of documents not then available, there had begun that movement toward a friendlier intercourse which has since been the predominating character-istic of British-American relations.

Within a year after the close of the war of 1812, James Monroe, American Secretary of State, in-formed the American Minister at London that the British Government seemed disposed to increase its forces on the Great Lakes, but added: the President authorizes me to

propose to the British Government such an arrangement respecting the naval force to be kept on the Lakes by both governments as will demonstrate their peaceful policy and secure their peace. He is willing to confine it on each side to a certain moderate number of armed vessels, and the smaller the number the more agreeable to him; or to abstain altogether from an armed force beyond that used for the revenue.

From that frank advance, came the Rush-Bagot agreement by virtue of which competitive armament on the Great Lakes was permanently avoided. It was the spirit of that suggestion, and the ensuing negotiations, which gave to the world the matchless object lesson of 4000 miles of frontier between America and Canada, forever unmarred by hidden mine or frowning bastion.

From the success of disarmament on the Great Lakes one may safely entertain the hope that, when other nations come as near to uniform standards of conduct as did Great Britain and America—with all their minor differences—world disarmament will be, not the vague dream of cloud dwellers, but a programme of practical statesmen amenable to facts.

Chapter VI

THE MONROE DOCTRINE;
ISOLATION AS A SUBSTITUTE FOR WAR

The logic of self-defence follows no set rules either Aristotelian or Baconian. It is frankly teleological, with the emphasis upon results, rather than upon the methods by which those results are attained. The Monroe Doctrine is and has always been a defensive policy, aiming at the safety of the independence which has cost the American Continents two hundred years of conflict.

When Europe was predominantly under the control of autocratic governments, the logic of self-defence led the President of the United States to warn all European nations that the United States would regard any attempt to extend Europe's system to any portion of the Western Hemisphere as dangerous to her peace and safety. And in like manner, when Europe altered its political machinery and established governments, popular in character, the logic of self-defence still insisted that any attempt to extend the political control of these governments to any portion of the Western Hemisphere would be similarly regarded. America, in the interest of her peace, is opposed to the near approach of democratic Europe, or of Bolshevic or Fascist Europe. And now that Japan has become in effect a European power, any attempt on her part to extend political control to any portion of the American Continents would be similarly opposed.

Political isolation has been viewed by America, from the first, as the indispensable prerequisite of her peace. The Monroe Doctrine therefore means that America deems political isolation a substitute for war. It says, as plainly as words intentionally vague can say it: "once open the Western Hemisphere to European political expansion and wars will come; keep that hemisphere closed to such expansion, and America may hope for a maximum of peace."

Amid changing policies, expanding trade, vast industrial development, and ever-increasing world contacts, this policy has remained written on the heart of America: and America has accepted the logical corollary, the political golden rule, "Do unto Europe as we would that Europe should do unto us."

The essential principles, which Monroe brought together in his message of December 1823, were old when he assembled them in that document. Before the American Revolution against Great

Britain, Alexander Hamilton wrote: "It ought to be the aim of American statesmanship to prevent and frustrate for all time European interference with the development of the States, and even with the destinies of the whole northern continent."

In this statement, Hamilton, then an open and ardent believer in constitutional monarchy, was not seeking a way to make America safe for democracy. He was merely formulating a policy designed to enable America to keep what she had, so as to be free to make it what she should later wish to make it. Yet, he wrote into history, clearly and unmistakably, one of the cardinal principles of the Monroe Doctrine, though applying it only to North America.

In 1776, Tom Paine formulated a second principle of the Monroe Doctrine: "As Europe is our market for trade, we ought to form no partial connection with any part of it. It is the true interest of America to steer clear of European contentions."

On March 23, 1793, Thomas Jefferson, then Secretary of State, wrote to Messrs Carmichael and Short, Ministers to Spain: "It is intimated to us... that France means to send a strong force early this spring to offer independence to the Spanish-American colonies....Interesting considerations require that we should keep ourselves free to act in this case according to circumstances."

These three principles, interpreted in the light of the dangers which America's alliance with France had made clear, and combined with a lofty idealism, formed the basis of the two thousand words into which Washington, in his Farewell Address, compressed his views upon the problem of defence against what he termed "the insidious wiles of foreign influence." His first thought, here as always, was of justice and peace:

Observe good faith and justice toward all nations; cultivate peace and harmony with all; religion and morality enjoin this conduct; and can it be that good policy does not equally enjoin it? It will be worthy of a free, and enlightened, and, at no distant period, a great nation, to give to mankind the magnanimous and too novel example of a people always guided by an exalted justice and benevolence.

But allegiance to "exalted justice and benevolence" implies to American minds Jefferson's principle of 1793, "that we should keep ourselves free to act...according to circumstances," for no man and no nation may say in advance of the circumstances, just where exalted justice is to be in a future controversy. The service of exalted justice demands free will, whether we speak in terms of individuals or of nations. Treaties which bind the nation to take one side, and bind it before the circumstances of the case are revealed, are but blind deeds of trust given to consciences not our own. The nation that vows service to exalted justice must be in the world, not apart from it; but she must also, to quote Washington's later words, keep herself free to "chose peace or war, as our interest, guided by justice, shall counsel."

Therefore, the second great principle of the Farewell Address follows: "It is our true policy to steer clear of permanent alliance with any portion of the foreign world." Temporary alliances for specific purposes had no terrors for Washington, for he added, "We may safely trust to temporary alliances for extraordinary emergencies." His caution was against implicating "ourselves, by artificial ties, in the ordinary vicissitudes of her (Europe's) politics, or the ordinary combinations and collisions of her friendships or enmities"; and his aim was to keep his nation free to respond to the call of "exalted justice and benevolence" from whatever quarter the call might come. Subject to these restrictions, he recommended "a liberal inter-course with all nations," and "temporary alliances" when the cause of justice demands them.

It is well to observe that the phrase "entangling alliances" formed no part of Washington's Farewell Address. His phrases were far more definite, "permanent alliances," on the one hand, which he wished his nation to avoid, and "temporary alliances," on the other hand, which he deemed a proper expedient "for extraordinary emergencies." The vague phrase "entangling alliances," is the phrase of Jefferson, who in his first Inaugural Address, wrote "Peace, commerce and an honest friendship with all nations, entangling alliances with none."

Clear as were the principles of defence by isolation and non-intervention in European affairs, to the minds of American statesmen, they had as yet been formulated with reference to the Northern Continent alone. But when Napoleon placed his brother on the Spanish throne (in 1808), the Spanish-American colonies in South and Central America and Mexico threw off their Spanish allegiance, only to return to it when the old Monarchy was restored in 1814. But the interval of open trade with all the world had widened their vision of what freedom might mean, and in 1816 when Spain again imposed her colonial system of restriction and exploitation, they rebelled again; and this time rebellion ripened into revolution; for they maintained their independence.

At the time of the first rebellion, President Jefferson wrote to the Governor of Louisiana: "We consider their interests and ours the same, and that the object of both must be to exclude all European influence from this hemisphere." But this statement was not a threat against existing European establishments on the Western Hemisphere since, from first to last, America refused to interfere with Spain's attempt to reconquer her American colonies. Already America was consciously committed to the policy which Monroe's message later formulated in the words: "With the existing colonies or dependencies of any European power we have not interfered and shall not interfere."

With American sympathy, then, but without American aid, the Spanish American colonies maintained their independence. By 1822, revolutionary governments had been established in every one of Spain's American colonies; and in that year, chiefly through the influence of Henry Clay, the United States recognized these colonies as independent Sovereignties. The Western Continents had become democratic, at least in profession of faith: and the problem of the United States was now bi-continental.

Not in a spirit of crusading altruism, but again

in the search for a sound method of self-defence, did the United States face this new aspect of an old problem. And the need of a sound method of self-defence had already become apparent. On September 26, 1815, Austria, Russia and Prussia had concluded at Paris a permanent alliance, calling itself Holy. This alliance, the offspring of the romantic mysticism of the Baroness de Krüdener, and of Czar Alexander I's remorse for complicity in the murder of his father, had proved most unholy from the point of view of the safety of free governments in the world. Its aim was the restoration of autocracy, first in Europe and then throughout the world. As definitely as the United States was committed to the task of making the Western Hemisphere safe for democracy, so definitely was the Holy Alliance committed to that of making the world safe for autocracy.

In 1820, the Holy Alliance cautiously invited the United States to become a member: to which John Quincy Adams, Secretary of State, answered:

"To stand in firm and cautious independence of an entanglement in the European system has been the cardinal point of their policy under every administration of their government, from the Peace of 1783 to this day." "For the repose of Europe as well as of America," he added, "the

European and American political systems should be kept as separate and distinct from each other as possible."

At first, England's regent had given his informal adhesion to the Holy Alliance; but, as the latter's reactionary purposes became apparent, his attitude became one of strong disapproval, which rapidly approached hostility. When the Alliance issued from Laybach its joint manifesto declaring, in the name of Christ, its purpose to put an end to all governments established by "any pretended reform effected by revolt and open force," Great Britain's hostility increased: and when, after deliberation at Verona, in October 1822, it declared its intention to "put an end to the system of representative governments," England cast about for a convenient method of thwarting the scheme.

At this point the British Foreign Secretary, Lord Castlereagh, was succeeded by George Canning, who promptly warned the American Minister at London, Richard Rush, that the South American republics were in danger, and intimated that British sympathy was with America's desire to keep the Holy Alliance from intervention in South American affairs.

Before the imperative necessity of action against the Holy Alliance arose, however, there emerged

another form of menace. Russia, from her foot-
hold in Russian Alaska, began to push southwards,
threatening, by the extension of her colonial possessions, the future of Oregon and California. To
John Quincy Adams fell the duty of warning
Russia that such extension was regarded as in-
imicable to the safety of that future which the
United States meant to safeguard. Thus, there
emerged the fourth essential element in what was
later to be called the Monroe Doctrine, for in his
correspondence with the Russian Minister, Baron
Tuyl, Adams declared that his Government was
resolved to "assume distinctly the principle that
the American continents are no longer subjects
for any new European colonial establishments."
This warning proved sufficient to check, for the
moment, the new method of menacing the security
of representative government on the American
Continent: for, as Adams later declared, "the
government of Russia has never disputed these
positions, nor manifested the slightest dissatisfac-
tion" concerning them.

Thus, before the beginning of the year 1823,
the four basic policies which were later combined
into what is now known as the Monroe Doctrine
had been developed and officially announced. The
American people were ready to maintain:

1. That no European nation should be permitted to interfere with and control the destinies of any American State, not already under European control.

2. That America would not interfere with the internal affairs of any European State.

3. That in international affairs America would hold herself free to act, or to refrain from action, "to chose peace or war, as our interest, guided by justice, shall counsel."

4. That the American continents are no longer subjects for any new European colonial establishments.

How far Great Britain sympathized with these policies appeared, on August 20, 1823, when George Canning placed in the hands of Richard Rush the following definite proposals:

"Is not the moment come when our governments might understand each other as to the Spanish-American colonies? And if we can arrive at such an understanding, would it not be expedient for ourselves, and beneficial for all the world, that the principles of it should be clearly settled and plainly avowed? For ourselves, we have no disguise.

1. "We conceive the recovery of the colonies of Spain to be hopeless.

137

2. "We conceive the question of recognition of them as independent states, to be one of time and circumstances.

3. "We are, however, by no means disposed to throw any impediment in the way of an arrangement between them and the Mother Country by amicable negotiation.

4. "We aim not at the possession of any portion of them ourselves.

5. "We could not see any portion of them transferred to any other power with indifference.

"If these opinions and feelings are, as I firmly believe them to be, common to your government with ours, why should we hesitate mutually to confide them to each other, and to declare them in the face of the world?

"If there be any other European power which cherishes other projects, which looks to a forcible enterprise for reducing the colonies to subjugation, on behalf of or in the name of Spain, or which meditates the acquisition of any part of them to itself, by cession or conquest," he added, "such a declaration on the part of your government and ours would be at once the most effectual and the least offensive mode of intimating our joint disapprobation of such projects....I am persuaded there has seldom, in the history of the world, occurred an opportunity when so small an effort of two friendly governments might produce so unequivocal a good, and prevent such extensive calamities."

Here was no call for a permanent alliance against which Washington had warned, nor for an entangling alliance, which Jefferson had denounced. It was the suggestion of the freest of European nations to the freest of American nations that they let the world know that their ideas were identical, their purposes the same. Rush's answer is significant. "I believe I may confidently say that the sentiments unfolded in your note are fully those which belong also to my government."

When the papers relating to these conversations reached President Monroe, he sent them to Ex-President Jefferson, asking his opinion:

"Many important considerations," he said, "are involved in this proposition. First, shall we entangle ourselves at all in European politics?... Second, if a case can exist, in which a sound maxim may and ought to be departed from, is not the present instance precisely that case? Third, has not the epoch arrived when Great Britain must take her stand either on the side of the monarchies of Europe, or of the United States, and, in consequence, either in favour of despotism or of liberty, and may it not be presumed that, aware of the necessity, her government has seized on the present occurrence, as that which it deems the most suitable, to announce and mark the commencement of that career? My own impression is that we ought to meet the proposal of the British government."

Jefferson's reply was an eloquent plea for the fullest acceptance of Canning's proposal of a joint British-American movement to thwart the Holy Alliance.

"The question presented by the letters you have sent me," he wrote to Monroe, on October 24, 1823, "is the most momentous which has ever been offered to my contemplation since that of independence. That made us a nation, this sets our compass and points the course we are to steer through the ocean of time opening on us. And never could we embark on it under circumstances more auspicious. Our first and fundamental maxim should be never to entangle ourselves in the broils of Europe; our second, never to suffer Europe to intermeddle with cis-Atlantic affairs.

"America, North and South, has a set of interests distinct from those of Europe, and peculiarly her own. She should therefore have a system of her own, separate and apart from that of Europe."

There follows a frank explanation of why he fears entanglement in European affairs: "While the last is labouring to become the domicile of despotism, our endeavour should surely be, to make our hemisphere that of freedom."

"One nation, most of all," he added, "could disturb us in this pursuit; she now offers to lead, aid, and accompany us in it. By acceding to her proposition we detach her from the band of despots, bring her mighty weight into the scale of free government, and emancipate a continent at one stroke, which might otherwise linger long in doubt and difficulty. Great Britain is the nation which can do us the most harm of any one, or all on earth; and with her on our side we need not fear the whole world. With her, then, we should most sedulously cherish a cordial friendship; and nothing would tend more to knit our affections than to be fighting once more, side by side in the same cause. Not that I would purchase even her amity at the price of taking part in her wars.

"But the war in which the present proposition might engage us, should that be its consequence, is not her war, but ours. Its object is to introduce and establish the American system, of keeping out of our land all foreign powers—of never permitting those of Europe to intermeddle with the affairs of our nations. It is to maintain our own principle, not to depart from it. And if, to facilitate this, we can effect a division in the body of the European powers, and draw over to our side its most powerful member, surely we should do it. But I am clearly of Mr Canning's opinion, that it will prevent instead of provoking war. With Great Britain withdrawn from their scale and shifted into that of our two continents, all Europe combined would not undertake such a war, for how would they propose to get at either enemy without superior fleets? Nor is the occasion to be slighted which this proposition offers of declaring our protest against the atrocious violations of the rights of nations by the interference of any one in the internal affairs of another, so flagitiously begun by Bonaparte, and now continued by the equally lawless alliance calling itself Holy."

After pausing to confess: "I have ever looked on Cuba as the most interesting addition which could ever be made to our system of States," and regretfully bidding the vision farewell in his assent to the self-denying clause of the Canning proposition, Jefferson adds: "I could honestly, therefore, join in the declaration proposed, that we aim not at the acquisition of any of these possessions."

From the author of the Declaration of Independence, the godfather of the French Revolution, and of the ill-fated experiment with economic pressure as a substitute for war, this letter is nothing less than astounding. Jefferson was advocating close co-operation with Great Britain, with the grave possibility of war in consequence; and in such a war America would have been against France.

As requested by the President, Jefferson asked Madison's opinion, which was sent to Monroe, under date October 30, 1823, and was as clearly in favour of the joint declaration as Jefferson's had been. "With that co-operation," wrote Madison, "we have nothing to fear from the rest of Europe, and with it the best assurance of success to our laudable views. There ought not, therefore, to be any backwardness...in meeting her in the way she has proposed."

It has long been the habit of historians to dismiss Madison's assent with the customary phrase, "Madison also spoke," and the impression left upon the mind is that, as compared with the ardour of Jefferson, Madison was but a lukewarm advocate of the proposed measure. It is true that there appears in Madison's letter a certain distrust of British motives which is absent from the more eloquent plea of Jefferson: but this is more than counterbalanced by the fact that Madison actually suggested that Monroe "invite the British Government to extend the 'avowed disapprobation' of the project against the Spanish colonies to the enterprise of France against Spain herself, and even to join in some declaratory act in behalf of the Greeks"; and that he frankly recognized that this would imply America's willingness "to follow it up by war."

It is doubtful whether, in all American history, it would be possible to find a proposition, comparable in importance, to which was given such complete and unequivocal assent by three equally seasoned statesmen, as Monroe, Jefferson and Madison gave to the proposition of accepting Canning's suggestion and issuing a joint British-American manifesto against the plans of the Holy Alliance. Had this been done at this time, the Monroe Doctrine would have been from the first moment the joint policy of two nations, placing them apart as the world champions of the cause of making the Western Hemisphere safe for democracy.

The inevitable question here arises, why then was the course proposed by Canning not taken? The answer is evident: Fear, suspicion, distrust, again the sinister triad which has wrecked so many fair prospects looking to the peace of nations. John Quincy Adams' *Memoirs*, under date November 15, 1823, thus records them: "Mr Madison's opinions are less decisively pronounced (than Mr Jefferson's), and he thinks, as I do, that this movement on the part of Great Britain is impelled more by her interest than by a principle of general liberty." Americans of that generation, and to a less extent it is true of later generations also, had been trained to distrust Great Britain. Indeed, it is not too much to say that they, like the people of all nations, had been trained to distrust all other nations, and to ascribe national virtue to themselves alone. In a conspicuous section of his Farewell Address, Washington had summed up this teaching in the words: "There can be no greater error than to expect, or calculate upon, real favours from nation to nation. It is an illusion which experience must cure, which a just pride ought to discard." The twentieth century has outgrown that doctrine: and is proceeding upon the belief that the experience of a century has not cured, but confirmed the 'illusion.' It is in this faith that we are able to hope that the slow but certain processes of evolution are developing an international conscience, without which all dreams of a world operating peacefully under International Law are but dreams.

Local minds think local thoughts: but the minds which point the path to lasting peace are those that lay hold on universal laws. Despite the drastic legislation which adorns the statute books of some States, otherwise judicious, America believes that evolution is a real process, and that it applies to the consciences of nations as well as to the bodies of men. When we think of that scene in far-off Cuba, a rich land, America's by conquest, where the Stars and Stripes fluttered for a moment in the southern breeze, and then descended voluntarily, to make place for the Lone Star flag of a new Republic to which America had shown the way of life, politically, we cannot doubt that, however truly America still believes most of the great lessons of Washington's Farewell Address, she does not believe that there is no such thing as international altruism.

The Monroe Doctrine was not formulated by the President whose name it bears. John Quincy Adams composed the stern paragraphs which announced, on December 2, 1823:

First: To all the world: "The American Continents, by the free and independent condition which they have assumed and maintained, are henceforth not to be considered as subjects for future colonization," and "With the existing colonies or dependencies of any European power we have not interfered and shall not interfere."

Second: To the Holy Alliance: "We should consider any attempt on their part to extend their system (earlier described as 'essentially different ...from that of America') to any portion of this hemisphere as dangerous to our peace and safety."

Third: To all Europe: "In the wars of European powers, in matters relating to themselves, we have

never taken any part, nor does it comport with
our policy so to do": but "with the movements
in this hemisphere, we are of necessity more immediately connected....We could not view any
interposition for the purpose of oppressing them,
or controlling, in any manner, their destiny, by
any European power, in any other light than
as the manifestation of an unfriendly disposition
towards the United States."

These simple, general, and conveniently vague
phrases represent all that was declared of the
principles which Canning had asked to have
"clearly settled, and openly avowed"; and they by
no means dominate the message. Of the thirteen
printed pages which the document contains,
paragraphs aggregating only two pages touch upon
foreign affairs; and the sentences now famous as
the Monroe Doctrine are scattered, disorganized
and almost buried in a mass of material relating
chiefly to domestic problems.

It is interesting to note how many of Canning's
suggestions, upon all of which Monroe, Jefferson
and Madison were agreed, appear in the message.

1. Canning: "We conceive the recovery of the
colonies of Spain to be hopeless."
Monroe: "It must be obvious that she (Spain)
can never subdue them."

2. Canning: "We conceive the question of recognition of them, as independent states, to be one of time and circumstance."

Monroe: "We have, on great consideration, and on just principles, acknowledged" them.

3. Canning: "We are, however, by no means disposed to throw any impediment in the way of an arrangement between them and the Mother Country by amicable negotiation."

Monroe: "In the war between these new governments and Spain, we declared our neutrality at the time of their recognition, and to this we have adhered, and shall continue to adhere, provided no change shall occur, which, in the judgment of the competent authorities of this Government, shall make a corresponding change on the part of the United States indispensable to their security."

4. Canning: "We aim not at the possession of any portion of them ourselves."

Monroe: "With the existing colonies and dependencies of any European power we have not interfered, and shall not interfere."

5. Canning: "We could not see any portion of them transferred to any other power with indifference."

Monroe: "It is equally impossible...that we should behold such interposition, in any form, with indifference."

From such a comparison it is evident that while America was formulating her policy of defence,

Great Britain, intent upon her own safety, had reached conclusions startlingly similar: and its proclamation was therefore received in England with enthusiasm. Mr Brougham declared in Parliament that no event had ever created greater joy among all free men of Europe, and that the message caused him to feel pride in the fact that he was connected by blood and language with the people of the United States. Rush wrote, "When the message arrived in London, the whole document excited great attention. It was upon all tongues: the press was full of it. The Spanish-American securities rose in the stock market, and the safety of the new States from European coercion was considered no longer doubtful."

Canning, while disappointed that his proposal of a joint declaration had been rejected, and quite out of sympathy with the idea that the United States could close to colonization two whole Continents consisting chiefly of unoccupied land, accepted the situation; but, with an eye to Great Britain's future interests, at once planned to forestall certain possible developments which he feared. Suspicion caused him to believe that, unless Great Britain should promptly recognize the South American States, America would proceed to organize them against Europe. In announcing the coming British recognition to the British Ambassador at Paris, on December 14, 1824, he declared: "The deed is done. The nail is driven... Spanish America is free, and if we do not mismanage our affairs sadly, she is English." He confessed that his recognition of the South American States was due to the fear that, without it, the United States might be able to bring about: "a division of the world into European and American, Republican and Monarchical, a league of worn-out governments on the one hand, and of the youthful, stirring nations, with the United States at their head, on the other."

From the point of view of Canning's fear, there is justice in the suggestion made by Professor Mowat, in his *Diplomatic Relations of Great Britain and the United States*, that Canning's much quoted boast: "I called the New World into existence to redress the balance of the Old," should read: "I called South America into existence to redress the balance of the North." But, had Canning been able to read the entire correspondence, now available to everyone, and to interpret it as time has interpreted it, he would scarcely have felt it necessary to do either. His fears, though reasonable, in view of his necessarily incomplete knowledge of America's real aims, were at least as groundless as the suspicions which had caused the United States to reject his proposition of a joint declaration. In this instance, as in so many others, there is illustrated the truthfulness of the observation of A. G. Gardiner, that in British-American relations "half knowledge has always produced whole friction, and whole knowledge left no friction at all."

It soon became apparent that, in her efforts to escape the Scylla of complicity in European affairs, the United States might find herself caught in the Charybdis of complicity in all the quarrels of the unstable South American States. To complete her defensive policy, therefore, it was necessary to define her own relationship to the South American Continent. In the spring of 1825 this opportunity came, after a bitter controversy as to whether the United States should or should not send representatives to a Congress of South American Republics to be held at Panama. After endless discussion, which need not be reviewed, Congress appropriated the money needed by the delegates whom President Adams had appointed, but defined their powers in the following resolution, dated April 18, 1826:

It is...the opinion of this House, that the government of the United States ought not to be represented at the Congress of Panama, except in a diplomatic character, nor ought they to form any alliance, offensive or defensive, or negotiate respecting such an alliance, with all or any of the South American republics; nor ought they to become parties with them, or either of them, to any joint declaration for the purpose of preventing the interference of any of the European powers with their independence or form of Government, or to any compact for the purpose of preventing colonization upon the continents of America; but that the people of the United States should be left free to act, in any crisis, in such a manner as their feelings of friendship toward these Republics, and their own honour and policy may at the time dictate.

Here then was the final, defining principle, whose declaration completes the Monroe Doctrine. This resolution, so harmonious with the principles already established to guide her relations with Europe, defined America's deliberate attitude toward South America. By its provisions, America stood alone and independent, free to act in any case, but equally free to refrain from action. Congress had reiterated, with respect to South America, what Washington's Farewell Address and Monroe's message had said with reference to Europe. With respect to both, America proposed to remain mistress of her own decisions, unfettered by

pledges, either of action or of inaction, whether
Europe or South America was concerned, keeping
ever in view her main objective, the security of free
government within the Western Hemisphere.

The Monroe Doctrine, effective for the immediate purpose of checking the crusade of the
Holy Alliance, and equally effective in many later
crises, has exercised a permanent influence both on
the American Continents and in Europe, but it
has never been employed to protect South American States from just punishment for international
misconduct. In 1838 the United States remained
unmoved while France blockaded Mexico, and
compelled the settlement of unsatisfied demands.
She watched without a flutter of the pulse while
Great Britain blockaded the port of San Juan de
Nicaragua in 1842, and again in 1844: while the
same power laid an embargo on the traffic at the
port of La Union, in 1851, and seized Brazilian
vessels in Brazilian waters in 1862 and 1863 in
punishment for the plundering of the vessel *The
Prince of Wales*. When in 1861 naval vessels of
England, France and Spain, sailed for Vera Cruz,
with the avowed intention of seizing Mexican
customs-houses and forcibly collecting the money
needed to satisfy their claims, the United States
still remained cold. But when, after the retirement

of England and Spain, France remained, filled with the ambition to realize in a new way her ancient ambition of a French empire upon the Western Hemisphere, that coldness vanished, and the United States formally notified the French Government that,

unless France could deem it consistent with her interest and honour to desist from the prosecution of armed intervention in Mexico, to overthrow the domestic republican government there existing, and to establish upon its ruins the foreign monarchy which has been attempted to be inaugurated in the capital of that country,

the traditional Franco-American friendship would be brought in imminent jeopardy.

In 1884, it was reported that Hayti contemplated transferring the peninsula of the Mole St Nicholas, or the whole Island of Tortuga, to France, and at once France was officially informed that such transfer would be in conflict with the "public policy known as the Monroe Doctrine." A few years later, in answer to a rumour that Great Britain intended to seize that same island, the American Minister in London was instructed to inform Downing Street that such action would be taken as a violation of the "well-known principles of the Monroe Doctrine."

The world has come to realize that the Monroe Doctrine has been a maker of peace. It admits that if South America had been divided into colonies, protectorates and spheres of influence, the god Mars would have reaped the chief harvest. At the Peace Conference at Paris, 1918–1919, America's representatives found no serious opposition to the general acceptance of its principles; and the Covenant of the League of Nations properly describes and recognizes it in the words:

Nothing in this Covenant shall be deemed to affect the validity of international engagements, such as treaties of arbitration or regional understandings like the Monroe Doctrine, *for securing the maintenance of peace.*

America's vital interests are safer under such recognition than they could be by the multiplication of regiments and battleships.

It is the self-denying principles of the Monroe Doctrine that have given it enduring life. Had it looked toward continental domination, continental exploitation, special privilege for the near and commercial exclusion for the more distant, it would not have outlived the generation which saw it formulated.

The self-denying principle and it alone can vitalize any combination of nations which forms to work for peace. The local thinker, the dreamer of a system which will give his nation special advantages, the believer in the divine right of muscles and a heavy hand, can never serve the cause of peace. He is looking backwards, and should be haunted by the dim memory of a certain pillar of salt on the plains of Sodom.

Chapter VII

A VISION POSTPONED

If one were seeking among American State-papers the paragraph which most adequately sums up her political ideals with reference to the treatment of other nations, he would turn to Washington's Farewell Address, Jefferson's first Inaugural Address, Monroe's famous message of December 2, 1823, Jackson's proclamation against nullification, Lincoln's two Inaugural Addresses and his Gettysburg speech, and to many other messages, addresses and public documents each of which breathes the spirit which has made Americans out of all races and kindreds and tongues.

Washington's Farewell Address, however, though magnificently interpreting ideals purely national, lacks the note of faith in international altruism which characterizes the America of to-day.

Jefferson's first Inaugural Address, also in lofty vein, is almost wholly local, its only recognition of the existence of other nations being found in the words: "Equal and exact justice to all men, of whatever state or persuasion, religious or political; peace, commerce, and honest friendship, with all nations—entangling alliances with none,"

and it emphasizes the grateful sense of responsi-
bilities bounded by national borderlines, in the
words: "Kindly separated by nature and a wide
ocean from the existing havoc of one quarter of
the globe;...What more is necessary to make us
a happy and prosperous people?"

Monroe's message was a timely weapon of defence, courageously employed to meet an emergency of international menace; but it represents a
refusal to co-operate with Great Britain in the
accomplishment of aims, clearly in the interest of
peace, and confessedly common to both nations.
Its words, "It is only when our rights are invaded
or seriously menaced that we resent injuries or
make preparation for our defence," interpret but
the primitive instinct of immediate self-defence.

Andrew Jackson's proclamation against nullification by South Carolina is a great interpretation
of a lofty nationalism, breathing an eloquence
which critics have refused to allow to the rough old
politician built on the lines of a man of war. But it
too speaks the language of a single sovereignty.

Lincoln's interpretations rise higher than any
of these: for his vision leaped the oceans, and his
mind thought instinctively in terms of universal
applicability. The eloquent sentences of his first
Inaugural Address pierce the international horizon

like shafts of light. His second Inaugural Address universalizes national experiences, and breathes the only spirit which can lead to lasting peace, the spirit of generous tolerance and forgiveness.

With malice toward none, with charity for all, with firmness in the Right as God gives us to see the Right, let us strive on, to finish the work we are in, to bind up the nation's wounds, to care for him who shall have borne the battle, and for his widow and his orphan, to do all, which may achieve and cherish a just and lasting peace among ourselves, and with all nations.

His Gettysburg speech is a requiem for all men who have given their lives in the service of human freedom: "We here highly resolve that these dead shall not have died in vain—that this nation, under God, shall have a new birth of freedom—and that government of the people, by the people, for the people, shall not perish from the earth."

But, above them all, in its grasp and formulation of the principles which should command all nations, in the world-wide intercourse which time has forced on all, stand the words in which President Cleveland denounced the nation over which he presided for the sin of which he held her guilty —the sin of plotting against the independence of a weak and helpless neighbour.

It has been the boast of our Government that she seeks to do justice in all things, without regard to the strength or weakness of those with whom it deals. I mistake the American people if they favour the odious doctrine that there is no such thing as international morality; that there is one law for a strong nation and another for a weak one, that even by indirection a strong power may with impunity despoil a weak one of its territory. ...The law of nations is founded upon reason and justice, and the rules of conduct governing individual relations between citizens or subjects of civilized states are equally applicable as between enlightened nations.

The considerations, that International Law is without a court for its enforcement, and that obedience to its commands practically depends upon good faith instead of upon the mandate of a superior tribunal, only give additional sanction to the law itself and brand any deliberate infraction of it, not merely as wrong, but as a disgrace. ...The United States, in aiming to maintain itself as one of the most enlightened nations, would do its citizens gross injustice, if it applied to its international relations any other than a high standard of honour and morality. On that ground the United States cannot be properly put in the position of countenancing a wrong after its commission, any more than of consenting to it in advance. On that ground it cannot itself refuse to redress any injury inflicted through an abuse of power by officers clothed with its authority and wearing its uniform.

Grover Cleveland is known in England, in so far as he is known at all, as the President who curtly dismissed Sir Lionel Sackville-West, the British Minister to Washington, and who later intervened in the Venezuelan boundary dispute. If one sought, therefore, a figure in American history who would be accepted on sight as "persona grata" by the British public, one would not turn to him: but President Cleveland, when he wrote the Venezuelan message, was neither playing politics, "twisting the Lion's tail," to use the language of the day, nor aiming to taunt Great Britain into war. He was but asserting, though in language harsh and undiplomatic, even provocative, the same abhorrence against what he conceived to be disregard of the sovereign rights of a weak nation as he had asserted against Germany in the case of Samoa in 1889, and later against the United States in the case of the Hawaiian Islands. And the language employed against his own country was harsher and more uncompromising than that which he used against either of the other two.

If we view the Venezuelan incident from the point of view of results, the outcome being what it was, there is now no reason for resentment on either side, but, on the contrary, much cause for rejoicing; since few incidents in history have proved more conclusively that war between the United States and Great Britain can never again be either necessary, wise, or beneficial; and that both nations are amenable to reason, and demand only justice, or what they deem justice. Between such nations the word 'war' may be regarded as but the echo of a foolish past.

The Venezuelan controversy was settled in the end by arbitration, and largely because Grover Cleveland was the progressive champion of arbitration. With his whole soul, he believed it to be the surest method of approximating international justice, and, where England was concerned, he advocated its adoption without stint or limit, even with reference to questions involving national honour. The all-too-general belief that a nation's honour is a modern Molech satisfied only by blood sacrifice, made no appeal to his supremely practical mind, and, from the beginning of his national career, he worked for the adoption of a general arbitration treaty with Great Britain, convinced that the method, once operative between those two nations, would be readily adopted by others, and thus slowly internationalize reason.

Furthermore, during President Cleveland's public life, both nations seemed ripe for the inauguration of such a system. As early as June 17, 1874, the American House of Representatives had unanimously recommended "arbitration as a rational substitute for war"; and in 1887, a memorial from two hundred and thirty-three members of the British House of Commons was presented to President Cleveland, expressing a desire that all future differences between the two nations be submitted to arbitration. In 1890, by unanimous vote of the American Congress, Benjamin Harrison, President between Mr Cleveland's two terms, was requested to open negotiations, in this sense, with all countries with which America was in diplomatic relation.

Thus, not only was it true, as Secretary of State Gresham reminded the American Ambassador to Great Britain in 1894, that "England and America are fully committed to the principle of arbitration" of specific controversies, but the project of a general arbitration treaty between the two countries was also well advanced in diplomatic negotiation, when in 1895, the Venezuelan incident suddenly menaced it with what seemed a threat of war.

But even before the latter incident was adjusted

by arbitration, Lord Salisbury had instructed the British Ambassador at Washington, Sir Julian Pauncefote, to renew the suspended negotiations with reference to a *general* arbitration treaty.

"In the spring of last year," Pauncefote's instructions declared, "communications were exchanged between your Excellence and the late Mr Gresham, upon the establishment of a system of international arbitration for the adjustment of disputes between the two governments. Circumstances, to which it is unnecessary to refer, prevented the further consideration of the question at that time.

"But it has again been brought into prominence by the controversy which has arisen upon the Venezuelan boundary. Without touching upon the matters raised by that dispute, it appears to me that the occasion is favourable for renewing the general discussion upon a subject in which both nations feel a strong interest....Neither Government is willing to accept arbitration upon *issues in which the national honour or integrity is involved*. But in the wide region that lies within this boundary, the United States desires to go farther than Great Britain."

This was a cautious renewal, in an hour of grave international tension, of a great theme, a suggestion demanding high political courage in view of the still-pending Venezuelan controversy, the in-

tense national resentment which President Cleveland's message had so recently aroused in England,
and the policy of "splendid isolation" which the
Salisbury government had followed.

The fact that, on the very day on which President Cleveland appointed his commission to in-
vestigate the Venezuelan boundary dispute, three
hundred and fifty members of the British Parliament signed a petition asking that henceforth *all*
British-American disputes be settled by arbitration
has caused some American writers to conclude,
not too generously, that Lord Salisbury was but
playing politics. The answer is obvious: If it was
politics, then thank God for nations where such
suggestions can serve as politics. Only supreme
faith in the peace-loving character of his nation
could lead a Prime Minister, in the midst of a contest like that over Venezuela, to propose, however
guardedly, a *general* arbitration treaty, the first of
its kind in history.

"A system of arbitration is an entirely novel
arrangement," Lord Salisbury told Pauncefote,

and, therefore, the conditions under which it
should be adopted are not likely to be ascertained
antecedently. The limits ultimately adopted must
be determined by experiment. In the interest of
the idea, and of the pacific results which are

165

expected from it, it would be wise to commence with a modest beginning, and not to hazard the success of the principle by adventuring it upon doubtful ground.

Lord Salisbury's letter, however, indicates the not unnatural belief that international courts, whether temporary arbitration tribunals, or permanent courts of international justice, will inevitably be biassed by patriotic attachments. The distinction, now so familiar to international relations, between the independent jurist who has been released by the advancing judicial conscience from the feeling that he must sustain his own nation, and the political representative whose constituents even yet expect him to "get something" for them, does not appear in his letters. On the contrary, he clearly doubted the possibility of securing an impartial court of arbitration for what he termed "*issues which concern the State itself considered as a whole.*"

"In the existing condition of international sentiment," he wrote to Sir Julian on March 5, 1896, "each great power could point to nations whose admission to any jury by whom its interests were to be tried it would be bound to challenge; and in a litigation between two great powers the rival challenges would pretty well exhaust the catalogue of the nations from whom competent and suitable arbiters could be drawn....By whatever plan the tribunal is selected, the end of it must be that issues in which the litigant states are most deeply interested will be decided by the vote of one man, and that man a foreigner...and he is sure to be credited, justly or not, with a leaning to one litigant or the other. Nations cannot afford to run such a risk in deciding controversies by which their national position may be affected or a number of their fellow-subjects transferred to a foreign rule."

Ambassador Bayard, however, on March 10, 1896, assured President Cleveland that the Prime Minister's distrust of the 'foreigner' did not apply to the United States.

"It is clearly his (Lord Salisbury's) belief," he wrote, "that a joint American and English Commission will be able to come to an agreement... (on the Venezuelan question). The case as stated by Great Britain is meant to be full and fair.... The desire of this Government to avoid the employment of a European arbiter at this time, will have great weight in inducing them to come to an agreement with the United States *alone*. I will not withhold from you my solicitude that this disposition for settlement should be strengthened by our own actions."

As the conversations between the Salisbury government and the Cleveland administration proceeded, it became evident that the former had misapprehended the situation when it had assured Sir Julian Pauncefote that "*Neither Government is willing to accept arbitration upon issues in which national honour or integrity is involved.*" Olney's replies, suggestions and contentions all combine to prove that the Cleveland administration was not only ready but eager to negotiate a treaty referring *all* questions of British-American controversy to final arbitration. He insisted that the proposed treaty should start with the presumption that *every dispute* should be arbitrated, rather than fought over. Whenever there was to be an exception recognized, he wished to have Congress or Parliament recognize it. Such a scheme, he argued,

puts where they belong the right and power to decide whether an international claim is of such nature and importance as not to be arbitrable, and to demand assertion, if need be, by force of arms. ...If war and not arbitration is to be evoked,... the direct representatives of the people, at whose cost and suffering the war must be carried on, should be properly charged with the responsibility of making it.

He was stoutly opposed to the idea that either the judges or the diplomats should be left free to decide whether or not arbitration would serve instead

168

of war. But he was far less suspicious of arbitration courts than was Lord Salisbury; far less disposed to question the possibility of securing an
international court which could be trusted to stand
clear of localism, that perennial enemy of international justice, and to think in terms of justice and
equity, rather than of special interests.

Those Americans who to-day insist that the
American Constitution forbids the treaty-making
power to recognize any court of final appeal save
the Supreme Court of the United States, should
ponder the words of Olney's reply to Pauncefote,
dated April 11, 1896:

It is hardly consistent with any reasonable
theory of arbitration that an award concurred in
by the arbiter of the defeated country should be
appealable by that country. It is obvious, too,
that the parties may properly be required to present all their facts and evidence to the original
tribunal. Otherwise, and if the award is appealable
in any event, the original tribunal might as well be
dispensed with, since each party will be sure to
make its real contest before the appellate tribunal
alone.

Neither Secretary Olney nor President Cleveland, however, was optimistic enough to believe
that even the best possible international court
would wholly avoid the lures of local thinking, and

Olney's pen phrased a principle as applicable to our generation as to his, in the words:

To insist upon an arbitration scheme so constructed that miscarriages of justice can never occur is to insist upon the unattainable, and is equivalent to a relinquishment altogether of the effort in behalf of a general system of arbitration. An approximation to truth—results which on the average and in the long run conform to right and justice—is all that the lot of humanity permits us to expect from any plan.

The American insistence upon universal, compulsory and final arbitration was so startling, so contrary to all tradition and practice, that the Salisbury Government stood aghast.

"The United States Government," wrote Salisbury to Pauncefote, on May 18, 1896, "wish that every claim to territory...shall go, as of right, before a tribunal or tribunals, of arbitration, save on certain special cases of an exceptional character, which are to be solemnly declared by the legislature of either country to involve the 'national honour or integrity'; and that any dispute once referred...to arbitration shall be decided, finally and irrevocably without the reservation of any further powers to either party to interfere. His Majesty's Government are not prepared for this complete surrender of their freedom of action.... Arbitration in this matter (manner) has as yet never been

obligatory. Claims by one neighbour to a portion
of the land of the other have hitherto been limited
by the difficulty of enforcing them. Hitherto, if
pressed to the end, they have meant war. Under
the proposed system, self-defence by war will, in
these cases, be renounced, unless the claim can
be said to involve 'the national honour and integrity.'"

Olney thus summed up the points of view of
the two nations:

Under the British proposals the parties enter
into an arbitration and determine afterwards, when
they know the result, whether they will be bound
or not. Under the proposals of the United States
the parties enter into an arbitration, having determined beforehand that they will be bound. The
latter is a genuine arbitration; the former is a mere
imitation.

He pointed out, furthermore, that Great Britain
was favouring "the practical exclusion of territorial claims from the category of proper arbitral
subjects," and admitted that, if all nations were to
be included in the treaty, to include such claims
might bring a multiplication of litigations: but as
between the United States and Great Britain alone,
he pronounced the danger "highly fanciful."

In short, Onley argued that as between Great
Britain and the United States there existed no

reason why territorial claims, like all other claims, might not safely be submitted to final, binding adjustment by arbitration. Indeed, he ventured farther, declaring that

"the condition of international law fails to furnish any imperative reason for excluding boundary controversies from the scope of general treaties of arbitration. If that be true of civilized States, generally,...it must be true of the two English-speaking nations," which have "not merely political institutions, but systems of jurisprudence, identical in their origin and in the fundamental ideas underlying them....The plan of Lord Salisbury...is that all the forms and ceremonies of arbitration should be gone through with, but with the liberty to either party to reject the award if the award is not to its liking....A proceeding of that sort must have a tendency to bring all arbitration into contempt."

The opinion of his own Government, Olney described as insistence that a nation "should decide to abide by an award before entering into arbitration, or should decide not to enter into it at all." And in justification of his contention, he might have added, as Carl Schurz later pointed out in defending the completed treaty, that in every one of the fourscore cases of international arbitration which the nineteenth century had witnessed, "the same spirit which moved the contending parties to accept arbitration, moved them to accept the verdict."

Clearly, while Great Britain's experience was the greater, the larger faith lay with the American government; since, not only did the Cleveland administration insist upon a treaty of general and universal arbitration between the two nations, but it likewise insisted that a majority award of the court be considered a final and binding award.

In the end, Lord Salisbury surrendered most of his misgivings, based upon long experience, to the optimism of the new Republic which had seen so little of the dark streams which run beneath the Chancelleries of Europe; but his correspondence shows that he would not have agreed to so sweeping an arbitration treaty with any other power on earth. The American government, in its turn, consented to certain limitations upon its ideal of "immediate, unlimited and irrevocable arbitration." But even as it stood, the treaty, as finally agreed upon, was an astonishing achievement.

The record of the conference between Sir Julian Pauncefote and Richard Olney is unfortunately very limited, as the final terms of adjustment between their positions were reached chiefly through personal conversations which were not

173

reduced to writing. But the treaty which was concluded and signed as preliminary to ratification
bound Great Britain and the United States to submit to final arbitration: "All questions in difference between them which they may fail to ad-
just by diplomatic negotiation," Mr Olney having
included even the pending Venezuelan question,
by the words: "No reason is perceived why the
pending Venezuelan boundary dispute should not
be brought within the treaty by express words of
inclusion."

Despite the famous instance of England's re-
pudiation of the Erskine treaty of 1809, America
had already learned to count with confidence upon
Parliamentary ratification of such treaties as the
British Foreign Office concludes: and in this case
Parliament ran true to form, by ratifying the
General Arbitration Treaty. It was wider in scope,
more generous in faith, more idealistic perhaps,
than the Salisbury Ministry had at first considered
advisable: but, it was held by them a step which
should not be refused; and Parliament agreed with
this opinion.

But in the case of treaties negotiated by America's
Chief Executive, there existed then, there exists
now, no such presupposition. In the history of
the United States, the Senate has proved the

burial place of many visions. In society, men have reckoned without their hosts, and without disaster: but no American Chief Executive has ever safely reckoned without the Senate in matters of foreign affairs. Secretary Hay once wrote: "A treaty entering the Senate is like a bull going into the arena. No one can say just how or when the final blow will fall, but one thing is certain—it (the bull) will never leave the arena alive." Henry Adams, in similar frivolous vein, spoke of Hay's own treaties as "hanging in the Senate like lambs in a butcher's shop."

When, therefore, Mr Cleveland sent his cherished General Arbitration Treaty to the Senate, on January 11, 1897, he was quite conscious of the possibility that it was going to its death, or to its mutilation. He knew that scores of treaties had been altered by the Senate after the Executive had accepted them, and that many more had been rejected. He knew also that of these mutilations and rejections, some had been eminently wise, some eminently unwise. Therefore his message transmitting the General Arbitration Treaty breathed hope rather than confidence:

"I transmit herewith," he said, "a treaty for the arbitration of all matters in difference between the United States and Great Britain. The provisions of the treaty, are the result of long and patient deliberation, and represent concessions made by each party for the sake of agreement upon the general scheme."

Frankly admitting that the treaty fell short of "immediate, unlimited and irrevocable arbitration of all international controversies," he declared it, nevertheless, "a long step in the right direction."

"It is eminently fitting as well as fortunate," he added, "that the attempt to accomplish results so beneficial should be initiated by kindred peoples, speaking the same tongue and joined together by all the ties of common traditions, common institutions, and common aspirations. The experiment of substituting civilized methods for brute force ...will thus be tried under the happiest auspices. Its success ought not to be doubtful.... The examples set and the lesson furnished by the successful operation of this treaty are sure to be felt and taken to heart...by other nations, and will thus mark the beginning of a new epoch in civilization."

This vision of a "new epoch in civilization," however, proved a vision postponed. Ardently as the Senate had responded to President Cleveland's Venezuelan message, proposing to determine the line between British and Venezuelan territory, "carefully, judicially," and then to enforce it, it showed no eagerness to join with him in accepting a peaceful adjustment for all similar disputes. The voice which then spoke had been a politically potential voice; but since the presidential election of 1896, it had become the voice of a man without a party. His "epoch-maker," was automatically referred to the Senate Committee on Foreign Relations, and, on February 2, 1897, it was favourably reported: but the end of the session was near, the inauguration of a Republican President only a month away, and the Senate, after prolonged debate, referred it back to the committee for further consideration.

In his inaugural address, President McKinley urged ratification in words as ardent as though he had himself negotiated the treaty. He declared that since arbitration

has been recognized as the leading feature of our foreign policy throughout our entire national history,...and since it (the Olney-Pauncefote General Arbitration Treaty) presents to the world the glorious example of reason and peace, not passion and war, controlling the relations between two of the greatest nations of the world, an example certain to be followed by others, I respectfully urge the early action of the Senate thereon, not merely as a matter of policy, but as a duty to mankind. The importance and moral influence of the ratification of such a treaty can hardly be over-estimated in the cause of advancing civilization.

But the voice of this Republican President, even when added to that of his democratic predecessor, proved not strong enough to secure the consent of the Senate. On March 18, the Committee on Foreign Relations again favourably reported the General Arbitration Treaty: but, on May 5, after a protracted debate, during which localism dominated, it was rejected, only forty-three Senators voting in favour of what Senatorial amendment had left. The project which two Presidents of opposite political parties had pronounced a step in the progress of advancing civilization thus passed out of history and was numbered among the innumerable things that might have been. Its defeat Olney declared "a calamity, not merely of national, but of world-wide proportions."

Since then there has been a noteworthy change in the methods of American Chief Executives, and one which might have saved the General Arbitration Treaty had it been employed. Cleveland, like most of his predecessors, held the view that the Constitution confines the Executive to the task of negotiating treaties, and presenting them to the Senate. Theodore Roosevelt, however, inaugurated, on a large scale, the practice of appealing, not only to the Senate, but to the Senate's master, public opinion. His philosophy of popular government embraced the belief that great advances can be made only when the public has been definitely aroused to their meaning. Cleveland would have scorned the suggestion that he should seek to save the treaty by a personal appeal to the public, even in the interest of the very great advance which it promised. Yet, in the light of subsequent developments, it seems likely that, had the people been informed of the issues at stake, had their enthusiasm been aroused by a careful campaign of public education such as that which had exposed the free silver heresy a few months earlier, the verdict of the Senate upon the General Arbitration Treaty might have been a different verdict. With a public opinion already predisposed to favour the extension of international arbitration, the task could hardly have been a difficult one.

The most vital element in an international understanding, because the only element which can give it power to bind, is the understanding of popular opinion. For a popular government incautiously to outrun public opinion in any great decision is to court disaster. Therefore, in the absence of any clear proof that the American people were ready for the acceptance of a general arbitration treaty with Great Britain, the Senate was perhaps justified in its attitude.

But that proof is no longer lacking. The history of the quarter of a century and more, which has passed since the Senate rejected Cleveland's General Arbitration Treaty, leaves little room for doubt that American public opinion, and that of the civilized world, hold verdicts of arbitration nearer to justice than verdicts won in battle. Their steady increase, and ready acceptance, itself constitutes a demonstration of this fact. Between 1900 and 1903, fifty-four controversies were adjusted between individual nations by arbitration, and since 1899, when forty-three nations, including Great Britain and the United States, established the Court of Arbitration at the Hague, fifteen cases have been voluntarily referred to it for arbitration and have been peacefully adjusted.

But despite such successes, undeniably great, with the days of world reconstruction has come the world-wide realization that the Hague Court of Arbitration is insufficient. The nations have therefore demanded and established a second international tribunal, called the Permanent Court of International Justice, which promises achievements beyond the power of mere arbitration;

and the most pressing international question before America to-day is this: Shall America adhere to this court also?

On January 23, 1926, Charles E. Hughes assured the American Bar Association that to answer this question in the negative would be "to reverse the American policy of a hundred years."

Of the truth of this statement there can be no question. Side by side with her advancing faith in arbitration has gone America's faith in the possibility of judicial adjustment of international controversies. Almost at the beginning of her national history, America's Supreme Court definitely accepted the law of nations, in the words: "When the United States declared their independence they were bound to receive the Law of Nations in its modern state of purity and refinement." This necessarily involves the decision as to the meaning of the law thus accepted; in other words, what *interpretation* of International Law is America bound to accept in her dealings with other nations, and what interpretation of International Law are other nations bound to accept in their dealings with her?

In attempting to determine the answer to this question two facts are beyond doubt: (1) America cannot properly insist that other nations obey

International Law as American courts interpret it. Modesty forbids such a position; and if modesty did not forbid, caution should; for it would be the most arrogant claim since the death of Caesar. (2) On the other hand, for America to stand bound to obey International Law as interpreted by tribunals on which she has no voice, would be to sacrifice her independence, to become an international ward in Chancery. It would place Congress in the absurd position of having the power and the consequent obligation to "punish offences against" a law of nations determined without America's co-operation, since America would still be bound, under the Supreme Court decision above cited, to "receive the Law of Nations in its modern state of purity and refinement."

William Edward Hall in a text book which has long been accepted by America as authoritative, defines the position of the American people— whether in the court or outside it—with precision, when he says: "They have lived and are living under (international) law, and a positive withdrawal would be required to free them from its restraints."

But logic is as pitiless as fate, and the logic of America's position renders the idea of such withdrawal particularly absurd. When seven Southern States declared themselves out of the Federal Union, and four others prepared to follow their example, President Lincoln declared, and the Federal armies enforced the view, that "No State, upon its own mere motion, can lawfully get out of the Union." The secession of the Southern States as the United States interpreted it had only served to place them "out of their proper, practical relation to the Union."

In like manner, no civilized nation can ever be freed from the obligations of International Law. The most that could be accomplished by America's "positive withdrawal" would be to put her "out of her proper practical relation" to International Law: or, as Sir Henry Maine puts it: "the State which disclaims the authority of International Law places herself outside the circle of civilized nations."

America, therefore, as a member of the Family of Nations, is equally under the obligations of International Law, whether she accepts or refuses membership in the Permanent Court of International Justice.

But from the moment when America's adherence to this Court was first proposed, there has been heard from Senators, Congressmen, from press, pulpit and platform, the insistent declaration that for America to adhere would mean the abandonment of her traditions, the end of her national independence and of her chance of peace. Most prominent among the arguments used has been the contention that the Constitution gives to the Federal Government no power to offer such adherence. "Among the delegated powers," writes one prominent editor, "..., is none that countenances the setting up of a judiciary superior in power to the Supreme Court. *It*, the Constitution made supreme, and it will remain supreme until the Constitution itself provides otherwise."

American history, however, justifies no such contention. From the very beginning of her national life, as has been shown, she has recognized and advocated the settlement of international disputes by arbitration: and arbitration is but the method of adjusting disputes by temporary tribunals. If therefore her government is competent to accept temporary tribunals, it is equally competent to accept permanent ones.

That she knew herself to be so competent is shown by the fact that in 1907 it was America's delegates who urged upon the Second Hague Conference the establishment of a Permanent Court of International Justice, with judges independent of all political control, and competent to decide international disputes according to the principles of the law of nations. The fact that the machinery for electing the judges could not be agreed upon prevented the execution of the suggestion at that time: but her subsequent relationship to the Hague Tribunal has firmly established the fact that America already accepts the decisions of courts which her Supreme Court is manifestly unable to reverse.

That the present representatives of the American people regard the argument of unconstitutionality as unjustifiable, was made clear on January 27, 1926, when the Senate of the United States, by a vote of 76 to 17, declared the United States ready to adhere to the Permanent Court of International Justice, subject to certain precautionary reservations, which reservations did not include a prior amendment to the Constitution.

The equally determined insistence that America should refuse adherence to the Court because of Washington's warning against "permanent alliances" is a *non-sequitur*. Washington's warning was against permanent *political* alliance, and the Permanent Court of International Justice is in no sense political. It is as different from a political alliance as the Supreme Court of the United States is different from America's political organizations. America is as suspicious to-day, as in Washington's day, of permanent political alliances: and her willingness to join the Permanent Court of International Justice is itself the proof of her conviction that the latter is a body non-political in character.

President Coolidge, on December 9, 1925, expressed this view, in the words: "It does not seem to me that any clause of the Statute confers on this Court authority political rather than judicial. ...We will be able to contribute largely to the progress of our own ideals by joining the other nations to secure and maintain such a tribunal."

There is a very sound reason for this careful distinction between judicial and political tribunals. In the slow evolution of the international conscience, the process has moved more rapidly on the judicial than on the political side. In the United States, a judge may be confronted with a case, in which one litigant comes from the judge's own State and one from some distant State: but no litigant feels that such a fact will endanger even-handed justice. The pressure of public opinion would drive from the bench a judge who would allow himself to be dominated by such motives. But the politician still too often devotes his talents to the problem of gaining special advantages for his village, his state or his nation, whichever happen to be his constituents, and is praised for his action. Therefore, Americans are ever readier to trust their interests to the discretion of courts than to the conferences of politicians.

And this larger faith in judicial institutions is not peculiar to America; it is very generally apparent, though not as yet universal. Judicial officers make with impunity decisions which political agents would hardly contemplate. In 1923, for example, the Tunis-Morocco nationality decree case was brought before the International Court, France and Great Britain being the litigants. The case involved one of the most delicate of international questions, that of domestic jurisdiction; but the French member of the court voted unhesitatingly with his colleagues, against the contentions of France. Furthermore, the opinion was thus made unanimous, when it need not have been, and the French judge on the court could have voted for France without fear of altering the opinion. Clearly he was confident that France, most nationalistic of nations, would not expect him to vote upon a judicial question as a national partisan.

But to-day as of old, the great enemy of international peace is the sinister triad: ignorance, suspicion and local mindedness; and the great enemy of these is the Court, which thinks in terms of justice, not of gain, and holds justice and equal law to be the right of all.

In her efforts to protect her citizens and her national rights, by peaceful methods, Great Britain, as well as America, has tried foreign alliance, negotiation, economic pressure and arbitration. Now both countries are ready to try judicial adjustment through a permanent court of international justice, preferring to abide by decisions of justice, rather than by decisions of the vast physical powers which are theirs.

The World's Pathway of Peace, once but a tangled lane, grows wider and clearer, as law supplants the primitive instinct to defend by slaughter. It has not yet become a broad highway: but, as we look back across the ages that have passed, we can see that despite all turnings it has followed one general direction, the direction which leads from war to law.

APPENDIX

THE motives which led to Napoleon's decision to sell Louisiana have been the subject of investigation for almost a century and a quarter: and still the historian is forced to rely upon speculation or doubtful inferences based upon documents many of which were evidently intended to mislead.

In a series of brilliant chapters in the second volume of his *History of the United States of America*, Henry Adams examines and rejects each of the usual explanations of Napoleon's conduct. Talleyrand's pious explanation, that among Napoleon's motives was "the wish to spare the North American Continent the war with which it was threatened," is manifestly out of character with the Conqueror whose god was Mars. "Fear of England was not," according to the same eminent historian, "the true cause." Napoleon, he adds, "had not to learn how to re-conquer Louisiana on the Danube and the Po. At one time or another Great Britain had captured nearly all the French colonies in the New World, and had been forced not only to disgorge conquests but to abandon possessions; until, of the three great European Powers in America, England was weakest. Any attempt to regain old ascendancy by conquering Louisiana would have thrown the United States into the hands of France." England knew, and Napoleon knew, that Talleyrand for once had spoken truth when, in his only literary production, a Memoir upon America and the Colonial system, he declared America wholly English both in tastes and commercial necessity, a land from which France could expect nothing. To suppose, as Napoleon pretended to suppose, that Pitt would be foolish enough to attack Louisiana under such conditions would have been to underrate the latter's wisdom, and that tendency was not among Napoleon's many weaknesses.

The desire for money was obviously not the controlling motive, for, as Adams points out, Manuel Godoy, the Prince of Peace, who had negotiated the American treaty of 1795, stood ready to pay the full price for Louisiana and keep it Spanish; and it is a matter of record that Jefferson had empowered his agents to pay ten million dollars for New Orleans and West Florida alone.

It is doubtless true, as Adams further declares; that "the real reason which induced Bonaparte to alienate the territory from France, remained hidden in the mysterious processes of his mind." But his further statement, "perhaps he could not himself have given the true explanation of his act," is less consistent with the Napoleonic character.

When we add the well-known facts, that, soon after his *coup d'état* of the 18th Brumaire, Napoleon had recalled Talleyrand to his old post of Minister for Foreign Affairs, conscious that his set purpose was that of confining America "within the limits which Nature seems to have traced for them"; that Napoleon refused to encourage Marbois in his suggestion that Louisiana when sold to the United States be given definite boundaries, adding cynically, "if an obscurity did not already exist, it would perhaps be good policy to put one there"; that he declared to Marbois: "we may hereafter expect rivalries among the members of the Union"; and that France had once before alienated Louisiana and then recovered it, giving at the time pledges which Napoleon had scornfully disregarded, it is at least reasonable to assume that he designed his cession to be merely a convenient method of guarding France's cherished American province until European victories should enable him to occupy it.

Furthermore, Napoleon had announced his own policy to his brother, Joseph, in the words: "within two years we shall be masters of the world." To assume, as historians have commonly assumed, that in the very act of preparing for the renewal of the war with England which was to open the way to the fulfilment of this vision, Napoleon abandoned for all time the vision of an American Empire which had inspired every Frenchman since the days of La Salle is to do small justice to the conqueror's faith in his own destiny.

The logic of proper inference looks rather to the supposition that he was merely setting the scenes for future action, and that, England disposed of, he would again seek to reclaim the lost province of Louisiana.

For EU product safety concerns, contact us at Calle de José Abascal, 56–1°, 28003 Madrid, Spain or eugpsr@cambridge.org.

www.ingramcontent.com/pod-product-compliance
Ingram Content Group UK Ltd.
Pitfield, Milton Keynes, MK11 3LW, UK
UKHW020316140625
459647UK00018B/1904